"*Snacking Bakes* is packed with Yossy's trademark crave-worthy sweet-and-salty, ooey-gooey excellence—all without the fussiness and dish pile-up in the sink. I dare you to flip through these pages and not immediately run to the kitchen to get started."

—**JENNY ROSENSTRACH,**
New York Times bestselling author of
Dinner: A Love Story

"Yossy's *Snacking Cakes* revolution was REAL, and I've got the butter-stained, marked-up recipe pages and happy cake-loving kids to show for it. And now we get cookies, bars, and more cakes that are just as low-maintenance? Yossy, we are not worthy!"

—**MOLLY YEH,**
New York Times bestselling cookbook author and Food Network host

"In no time at all, readers will be sliding flavorful, beautiful bakes in and out of their ovens as if they've been doing it forever—that's the magic of Yossy's simple, achievable collection of recipes: positively 100 percent bakeable—no skips!"

—**ERIN JEANNE McDOWELL,**
author of *The Book on Pie* and
Savory Baking

"Yossy knows something fundamental about all of us. When we want something sweet, we want it now. Her treats deliver. No fuss, just easy, accessible, truly inspired deliciousness. *Snacking Cakes* is well-worn, batter-spattered, and beloved. Our copy of *Snacking Bakes* is sure to be a mess in no time."

—**SAMANTHA SENEVIRATNE,**
author of *Bake Smart*

"Yossy has an amazing ability to make incredibly desirable recipes that are also incredibly simple to make. This wonderful book, which is packed full of reliable and ridiculously tasty recipes, is one you'll find yourself baking from time and time again."

—**EDD KIMBER**, baker and author of
One Tin Bakes Easy

"Yossy's new book is filled with simple, anytime bakes that cover all the sweet treat bases. Her use of pantry ingredients to create classic but unique flavor combinations is stellar, and you won't need any fancy equipment to make any of the recipes; the biggest challenge will be deciding what to make first. This book already has a permanent spot on my shelves."

—**SARAH KIEFFER**, author of
100 Cookies and *100 Morning Treats*

snacking bakes

snacking
bakes

Simple Recipes for Cookies, Bars, Brownies, Cakes & More

YOSSY AREFI

Photographs by Yossy Arefi

Clarkson Potter/Publishers
New York

contents

introduction

When *Snacking Cakes* was first published in the fall of 2020, I had no idea that it would have such a huge impact on the lives of everyday bakers. Since the recipes were so quick to make and didn't require much effort, equipment, or special ingredients, I heard from so many people who told me they cooked from *Snacking Cakes* more than any other cookbook they owned—including those who found themselves baking for the very first time (ever!), parents who made those cakes with their kids (or while their kids were napping), and lifelong bakers who relished being able to satisfy their sweet tooth on a whim.

It was clear that the promise of simple, anytime recipes should extend well beyond cakes—don't we deserve a bite of a rich fudgy brownie or warm, out-of-the-oven chocolate chip cookie just as easily? *Snacking Bakes* delivers just that. You'll find accessible, irresistible recipes for cookies, bars, brownies, and (more!) cakes that rely on basic pantry ingredients and no special equipment so you can make and enjoy a treat at a moment's notice. I've tried to anticipate and satisfy every sweet and salty craving in this collection, so there will be a little something for everyone. You'll discover chocolatey cakes, fruit-glazed cookies, gooey buttery bar cookies, brownies, and a lot more.

Plus, you'll find gluten-free and vegan recipes (marked by GF or V) or easily adaptable options in each chapter, so no one's left out.

If you are a beginning baker, you will love how simple and fast these recipes are—almost everything can be made in less than an hour, in one bowl. They are full of comforting familiar flavors like chewy peanut butter blondies and soft oatmeal raisin cookies, and hopefully some new and inspiring ones, too, like berries paired with tahini, malted milk powder added to perfectly chewy sugar cookies, and a savory bread filled with everything bagel seasoning and cream cheese that is irresistible warm. You can throw together a batch of cookies or a simple pan of bars on a weeknight or squeeze one in during naptime, and they are special enough that you'll want to share them with your friends and neighbors. And you can always skip the glazes and toppings if you like. There's an opportunity for more experienced bakers to take things to the next level by mixing and matching bakes and icings. Or make toppings like salted caramel, hot fudge, or strawberry sauce to turn your baked good into an ice cream sundae. Even though these recipes are easy, they certainly are not boring.

Although I have a relatively spacious kitchen for a New York City apartment dweller, whenever I post a picture of it online I inevitably get comments asking how I cook and bake in such a small space, with no dishwasher. I've made thousands of cookies and hundreds of cakes in my little galley kitchen, and it has helped me streamline my cooking and baking so much. I have made many labor-intensive "project bakes" over the years, but in my day-to-day I think twice before pulling out an additional bowl or set of tools to get a job done, and I love to pass those dish savings on to others. These are fun recipes for folks with tiny kitchens like mine and those who need an easy pick-me-up. At the end, you'll have a tasty treat and only a few items to wash instead of every bowl you own.

The book begins with the original snacking bake—the cookie. Cookies are one of the first things that a lot of folks learn to bake and for good reason. They often feel less intimidating than other desserts, and they are pre-portioned into perfect bites that fit in a lunchbox, picnic basket, or alongside your afternoon coffee or tea. Cookies should feel friendly and easygoing, like you can whip them up at any moment, and these recipes deliver on that exact promise. Not all cookies in the world are that easy, but these are: You'll never have to wait for butter to soften or get an electric mixer out. I'll also never ask you to refrigerate the cookie dough before you bake it, and if you have two large baking sheets, you can bake all of the dough in one go, no waiting around for multiple batches. Even though they're so simple, these cookies have a wonderful variety of flavors and textures and are anything but boring. From pat-in-the pan buttery shortbread that you can riff on so many ways to ooey, gooey, and chewy cookies like White Chocolate Macadamia Nut Cookies (page 74) filled with brown butter, or Snack Attacks (page 80) filled with sweet and salty mix-ins, to bright and lemony Blueberry Cornmeal Cookies (page 50), all of your cookie desires will be met.

Next up are the highly shareable (if you must), brownies and bars. These recipes are near and dear to my heart, drawing upon flavors that remind me of mornings grabbing a coffee and treat from the coffee cart when I tagged along to work with my mom, like Pink Cookie Bars (page 101) and Raspberry Mazurkas (page 108). My Midwestern in-laws were also a huge influence (folks in the Midwest are *serious* about their bars), and you'll see a range of flavors from buttery oat-filled bars to rich

and chocolatey cookie bars to spiced molasses bars topped with coffee glaze.

The bars and brownie recipes don't require an electric mixer either, and they're even easier than cookies because you can just throw the dough right into the pan, no portioning needed. Some of them are dressed up with a bit of glaze or frosting, while others are served straight up. As always, there's lots of room to make these recipes your own by switching up the toppings, spices, or mix-ins. All of the bars use your trusted 8 × 8-inch pan, but if you have a crowd to feed, you can always double the recipes and bake them in a 9 × 13-inch pan, with just a few more minutes of baking time.

There are even two cookie barks that you'll mix up, pat into a round, and bake on a sheet pan. Bake the cookie until matte, crisp, and golden. Then, use your hands to break the big cookie into whatever size pieces you need at the moment. Cookie barks are big crispy cookies for lazy people (like me!). Eat them as is or serve cookie shards with a scoop of ice cream and some fancy sauce (pages 182 and 183) for a super-quick and satisfying dessert.

The cake chapter picks up right where *Snacking Cakes* left off with lots more fun, simple cakes, mixed up in one bowl with minimal ingredients and minimal fuss, like Brown Sugar Peach Cake (page 170), Berry Bran Cake (page 148), and a seriously moist and tasty vegan Chocolate Banana Cake (page 153), topped with mocha glaze if you like. You'll find lots of ideas to customize these cakes, and you can always try your own spin, too!

I turn to baking in times of both stress and joy, and it has always been such a comfort for me. These recipes make it so easy to roll up your sleeves and make something delicious for when you want to celebrate a great day or zone out in the kitchen at the end of a tough one—even if you don't have that much time or energy to do it.

cravings matrix

GF Gluten-free
V Vegan

chocolatey	warm and toasty

COOKIES

chocolatey	warm and toasty
Banana Brownie Cookies **V** 77	Do-It-All Salted Butter Shortbread 46
Chocolate Chip Crispy Rangers 54	Magical Peanut Butter Cookies **V** 73
Chocolate Peanut Butter Brownie Cookies 36	Malted Sugar Cookies 44
Fudgy Sesame Oat Cookies 70	Salt and Pepper Olive Oil Shortbread **V** 78
Gluten-Free Chocolate Chip Cookies **GF** 66	Thick and Chewy Oatmeal Raisin Cookies 39
Malted Chocolate Cookies 59	Thin and Crispy Maple Espresso Cookies 49
Monster Cookies **GF** 40	White Chocolate Macadamia Nut Cookies 74
New Favorite Chocolate Chip Cookies 61	
Snack Attacks 80	
Thin and Crispy Chocolate Cacao Nib Cookies 69	
Vegan Chocolate Chip Cookies **V** 63	

BARS, BROWNIES, AND BARKS

chocolatey	warm and toasty
Brown Butter Chocolate Chip Cookie Bark 97	Banana Nut Blondies **V** 111
Chewy Cocoa Brownies 86	Coconut Cookie Bark 120
Chocolate Cherry Pistachio Bars 116	Coffee-Glazed Molasses Bars 112
Loaded Chocolate Chip Cookie Bars **V** 107	Date and Pistachio Coffee Bars 126
Pumpkin Chocolate Chip Bars 115	Ginger Cherry Oaties 104
Triple-Chocolate Olive Oil Brownies 123	Glazed Cookie Butter Bars 98
	Peanut Butter Blondies 119
	Pink Cookie Bars 101

CAKES

chocolatey	warm and toasty
Brown Butter Marble Cake 136	Cheesy Jalapeño Corn Bread 179
Chocolate Chip Snickerdoodle Cake 132	Cornmeal Carrot Cake **V** 139
Chocolate Prune Cake 165	Everything Bagel Bread with Scallions 180
Chocolate Ricotta Cake 143	Nutty Parsnip Cake 162
Mocha Banana Cake **V** 151	Peanut Butter and Jam Cake with Raspberries 135
Not Quite Texas Sheet Cake 157	Walnut Cream Cheese Coffee Cake 145

fruity

let's stock the pantry!

my hope is that you'll be able to pick this book up and make something to satisfy your snacking craving immediately, no grocery store trips required. That begins with a basic stocked pantry, but don't feel like you have to go out and buy everything all at once if you are starting from scratch. Begin with the easy stuff: flour, baking soda, baking powder, granulated sugar, brown sugar, powdered sugar, cocoa powder (if you like chocolate), vanilla extract, and a couple of spices like cinnamon and ginger. Then every time you have a few extra bucks in your grocery budget, you can add something new, like a bar of chocolate, malted milk powder, or espresso powder. (This is also a great way to build up your spice cabinet, just buying one or two things at a time.)

Let us also not forget the joy of the bulk bin! I have a tiny kitchen and don't stock every type of nut or dried fruit or chocolate in the world, so I often hit up the bulk bins at my local natural foods store to buy those ingredients in small (tiny!) amounts as I need them. You can buy a few tablespoons of what you need, usually pretty inexpensively, and investing in a few tablespoons of sliced almonds or sesame seeds will take your baking to the next level. Some stores even have bulk spices where you can pick up a little bit of cardamom or allspice or whatever you need. If you like it, you can then pick up a little more or a full-size jar next time you have some space in your grocery budget.

Baking Soda and Powder: These leaveners are what make cookies spread and brown and cause cakes to rise and give them a lovely fluffy texture. Yes, you'll need both baking soda and baking powder as they have slightly different ingredients and uses. Baking soda reacts with acidic ingredients like buttermilk to give your bakes lift and help them brown. Baking powder is a combination of baking soda and dry acid and is double-acting, which means that it is first activated when it is dissolved in liquid and then again when it is heated. Baking powder reacts with alkaline ingredients like Dutch process cocoa powder and recipes that do not have any acidic ingredients. It is also less powerful than baking soda, which is why you often see recipes that call for both.

If you haven't used your baking soda or powder in a while, you can test their freshness with the following methods:

- **Baking soda:** Stir a teaspoon or so into about ¼ cup of distilled white vinegar. It should bubble and fizz like an elementary school science fair volcano.

- **Baking powder:** Put a teaspoon into a heatproof container and pour about ¼ cup of boiling water on top. If it bubbles and fizzes, you are good to go.

Butter: Gone are the days of waiting for butter to soften to the exact right consistency. Call it impatience, or better yet, call it efficiency: These recipes are made with melted butter. Almost all of them call for your standard, run-of-the-mill grocery store unsalted butter, so you can stock up when it's on sale.

Chocolate: Sometimes a cute little chocolate chip is just what a recipe needs, while for others a chunky, chopped chocolate bar is the move. Chopped chocolate will melt, pool, and create delicious little puddles of goodness, especially in cookies, while chips contain stabilizers that will help them keep their shape, which we definitely want sometimes, too. When you're chopping chocolate for cookies, aim for pieces that are slightly larger than a chocolate chip, with some very fine pieces and a few larger pieces mixed in. The combination of sizes gives the cookies wonderful texture and flavor, especially the fine pieces that get mixed throughout the batter.

Cocoa Powder: The recipes in this book use Dutch process cocoa powder, which is processed with alkali. This gives the cocoa rich deep color and flavor. As a general rule, don't swap natural cocoa for Dutch process cocoa as they have different pHs and react differently with leaveners like baking powder and baking soda.

how to melt butter

This might seem obvious, but there is a bit of a trick to melting butter so you can use it right away. I don't have a microwave at home, so I melt butter in a small skillet or saucepan set over medium-low heat. You can also melt butter in a microwave in 20-second bursts.

Remove the butter from the heat (or from the microwave) when there is still a little bit of opaque, unmelted butter left in the pan or bowl. This will ensure that the butter doesn't get too hot and you will be able to work with it immediately, rather than waiting for it to cool. You can add the butter, unmelted bits and all, to the bowl when you start your recipe.

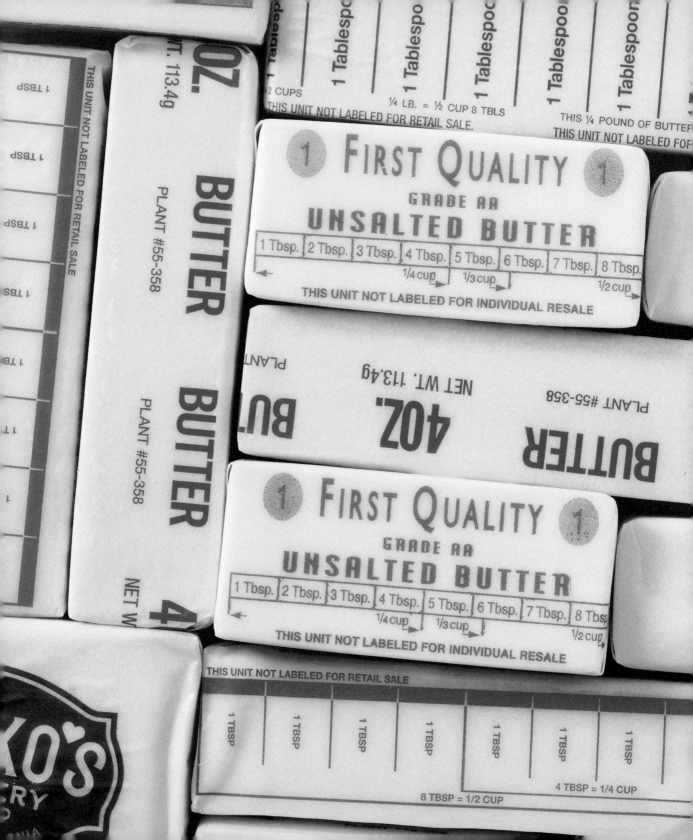

how to brown butter

There are a few recipes in the book that call for browning butter. Brown butter makes your cookies and cakes so supremely delicious you won't regret the little extra time and effort it takes to make it happen. Browning butter also reduces its water content, so in some of the recipes that call for brown butter we are going to add a little bit of cold butter back to the mix to ensure your bakes have the right texture. This also helps cool the butter down, win-win.

To brown butter, place it in a small skillet or saucepan with a light-colored interior and set it over medium heat. Once melted, cook the butter, stirring constantly until the milk solids are deep golden brown, about 3 minutes. It will foam quite a bit during this process, so don't be alarmed, but make sure to use a pan deep enough to accommodate the foam without boiling over.

TIPS

- Don't walk away during this process or your butter may burn on you; trust me, it happens quickly and it smells bad.

- I really like to do this in a ceramic nonstick skillet because all of the milk solids just slide right out of the pan; you may have to scrape a bit if you use a pan that does not have a nonstick coating.

- In cake and bar recipes you can generally substitute plain melted butter for brown butter. If a cookie recipe calls for brown butter, however, I don't recommend substituting melted butter as the moisture content will be slightly different and may affect the way the cookies spread.

Eggs: These recipes all call for large eggs, and it's okay (even preferred in the cookie recipes) to use them cold, straight from the fridge. They provide structure, moisture, and lift, depending on the recipe.

Flour: Unbleached all-purpose is the go-to flour for most of the recipes in this book, though a few recipes call for a whole-grain or nut flour to add flavor and texture. For my gluten-free friends, there are a variety of recipes that are naturally gluten-free. For the cakes and bars that are not naturally gluten-free, I've had great success with the 1:1 gluten-free flour blends that are so easy to find these days. Cookies can be a little trickier to swap in gluten-free flour because of the way that cookies spread, but definitely give it a try; just know that your cookies may look a bit different than the ones on these pages.

Instant Espresso Powder: This is a magical baking ingredient. It makes chocolate taste more chocolatey, its bitter edge can temper the sweetness of caramel, and it's a nice little rich background note to add to spice cakes and gingerbread. You might not taste the coffee flavor, but you will know there's a little something going on. If you buy one specialty item to up your baking game, this should be it!

Malted Milk Powder: Like the espresso powder, this is another favorite, versatile flavoring secret. It adds a caramelly, toasty, milky, malty flavor to all sorts of baked goods, from cookies to cakes. It pairs well with chocolate, vanilla, spice, and fruit flavors.

Milk: Milk is mostly used in these recipes to thin glazes and frostings; whole milk is preferred. That said, you can use whatever you have on hand, including unsweetened nondairy milk.

Nut and Seed Butters: Some recipes specifically call for creamy conventional peanut butter (I like Jif or Skippy), while others require natural peanut or almond butter, their less processed counterparts. For natural nut butters, make sure to stir in that oil that collects on the top before measuring. Because the two are so different, it is generally not a good idea to swap one for the other unless the recipe explicitly states that either will work.

Nuts: Most of the recipes call for toasted nuts as I find they just taste better that way. My preferred method is to spread the nuts in a single layer on a rimmed baking sheet, then pop them in the oven while it is heating and take them out when they are golden and fragrant. Timing will depend a little bit on how quickly your oven heats, but in mine, the toasting takes about 10 minutes. You may want to start checking a little earlier.

Oil: Many of these recipes use oil instead of, or in addition to, butter. Neutral oil is odorless and flavorless so it won't affect the flavor of your baked goods. It will add moisture to cookies and gives cakes a lovely soft texture. I recommend canola or grapeseed; avocado is also a great option but a little pricier. In recipes that call for olive oil, use a mild-flavored fruity olive oil rather than a grassy oil if possible. If you are wary of using olive oil in these cakes, since it's often associated with savory applications, you can certainly combine it with a bit of neutral oil. Olive oil pairs well with chocolate, citrus, and other fruits, so I encourage you to give it a try!

Powdered Sugar: This is used in a few ways in these recipes—as an ingredient in cookies to help make them crisp and tender, and sometimes in a glaze or frosting to top a treat. Organic and conventional powdered sugar can be used pretty interchangeably. Conventional powdered sugar is bright white and usually has cornstarch as an anticaking agent. Organic is made from sugar that is processed differently, so it is usually a bit creamier in color and sometimes uses tapioca starch instead of cornstarch as an anticaking agent.

Salt: This can be a tricky topic in cooking and baking because some salts are saltier by volume than others. For these recipes, I use fine sea salt. You can substitute an equal volume of table salt or Morton kosher salt. However, if you use a flaky kosher salt like Diamond Crystal (which I used in my *Snacking Cakes* recipes), increase the salt by 1½ times. So, for example, in a recipe that calls for ½ teaspoon fine sea salt, use ¾ teaspoon Diamond Crystal kosher salt.

Spices: Does your spiced cake taste bland and boring? High-quality, fresh spices are a baking game changer. I like to source spices from Penzeys, Burlap & Barrel, and Diaspora Co. For the best flavor, use your spices within about six months of purchase. If you don't bake a lot or don't have space to store lots of spice jars, your local supermarket or natural foods store might sell bulk spices so you can just pick up what you need in the short term.

Sugar: You can get by with plain white granulated sugar and light brown sugar for almost all of these recipes, but sometimes the deep molasses flavor of dark brown sugar is just the ticket. Light and dark brown sugars can be used pretty interchangeably, so don't worry if you have only one or the other. Turbinado and demerara sugars can be used interchangeably anytime I call for coarse sugar to sprinkle on the top of a baked good. Some refined sugar is processed using animal products, so for the vegan recipes I call for USDA-certified organic cane sugar, brown sugar, and powdered sugar. If that is not a concern, feel free to swap in their conventional counterparts.

Vanilla Bean Paste and Extract: Fruit, chocolate, spices, and nuts all pair well with floral, sweet vanilla, so you'll find it in quite a few of these recipes. The paste and extract can be used interchangeably 1:1, so no stress if you don't keep both stocked. The little flecks of vanilla seeds in vanilla bean paste are quite lovely, though, so I use the paste when I know they will take center stage. I love the products from Heilala and Nielsen-Massey.

bursts of flavor

These flavor-packed ingredients add tons of taste (without adding liquid, which can wreak havoc on a baked good), so feel free to add a teaspoon or two to whatever you are making to give it a little boost.

Citrus Zest: Lemon, lime, grapefruit, orange, I love them all to add brightness to fruity and spicy bakes.

Freeze-Dried Fruit: Fresh fruit adds moisture to baked goods, which sometimes isn't the name of the game, but a little bit of crushed freeze-dried berries can punch up a cookie dough or glaze or provide a little bit of fruity color or flavor to a rich cake.

Instant Espresso Powder: Coffee not only enhances chocolate flavor but it also pairs beautifully with toasted nuts, brown sugar, and vanilla.

Malted Milk Powder: This flavor-packed powder adds richness, toastiness, and even a little bit of saltiness to the background flavor of just about any baked good. You may not know exactly what it is when you taste a malted cookie or cake, but you'll know there is something delicious happening in the background. Try adding a couple of tablespoons to cake batter, frosting, or cookie dough.

Vanilla Bean Seeds and Extract: Vanilla is everyone's BFF in the baking world, and while it can definitely stand on its own, it can also enhance fruity and chocolate flavors. It also pairs well with warm spices and toasty flavors. You can add vanilla extract, paste, or seeds to just about any bake for a little additional flavor.

what about substitutions?

Butter: If you're avoiding dairy, vegan butter can generally be substituted for dairy butter in cakes and bars with good results. Individual cookies are a little trickier because the moisture content in vegan butters varies and can affect the way the cookies spread. I like Miyoko's Creamery and Earth Balance vegan butters. Buy the vegan butter that comes in sticks, rather than a tub. They are more reliable for baking because they come in unsalted versions, are easier to measure, and are not whipped like some butters that are sold in tubs.

Chocolate: Feel free to swap bittersweet for milk or semisweet chocolate and vice versa, but keep in mind the cookies will be sweeter if you choose a sweeter chocolate. Chocolate chips contain stabilizers to help them keep their shape, so generally you should stick to chips or chopped based on what the recipe calls for. For example, chopped chocolate bars will melt into gooey delicious puddles in cookies, which will affect the way cookies spread, so if you substitute chips they will spread less. Most of the cookie recipes call for chopped chocolate, and you can chop up either a chocolate bar (like the kind you would eat on its own as candy), callets, or feves.

Eggs: Egg replacements can work well in cakes but are less consistent in cookies and bars because they can cause some textural issues. If you'd like to try substituting eggs, two common vegan egg replacements are a "flax egg" or a "psyllium egg."

- Flax egg: 1 tablespoon finely ground flaxseed + 2½ tablespoons warm water. Stir and let sit until it gels.

- Psyllium egg: 1 tablespoon finely ground psyllium + 2½ tablespoons warm water. Stir and let sit until it gels.

Flour: In most recipes, you can substitute a whole-grain flour for one-third of the all-purpose flour. Gluten-free all-purpose flour blends work well in cakes and bars but are a little trickier in individual cookies because of the way they make cookies spread. My favorite gluten-free flours are Bob's Red Mill 1 to 1 Baking Flour, King Arthur Measure for Measure Flour, and Cup4Cup Multipurpose Flour.

Fruit: You can easily swap apples and pears. Citrus juices and zests can also be easily swapped one for the other. Grapefruit can tend toward bitterness, though, so keep that in mind if you are substituting it for lemon, lime, or orange. Berries are pretty easy to switch up, although sometimes baked strawberries get a little soggy, but you do you!

Milk and Buttermilk: Dairy and unsweetened nondairy milk can be used interchangeably. Buttermilk adds tang and tenderness, and it's one of my very favorite ingredients in cake, so I recommend picking up a small container next time you're at the store. However, in a pinch, you can mix 2 parts plain yogurt with 1 part milk. I do not recommend using lemon juice or vinegar stirred into milk to make "buttermilk."

Nuts: They are pretty interchangeable, so feel free to sub walnuts for pecans, or hazelnuts, or peanuts, or whatever you like.

Sour Cream and Yogurt: Sour cream and yogurt can be used fairly interchangeably, but sour cream has a higher fat content, and substituting it will change the richness of your bakes. If you are substituting a nondairy version, make sure to use an unsweetened one.

Spices: Warm spices such as cinnamon, nutmeg, ginger, and cardamom can be swapped one for one, although stronger spices like cloves and allspice should generally be used sparingly.

Sugar: Sugar performs an essential function in baking. I don't recommend reducing the sugar in baking cakes, cookies, or bars. Light and dark brown sugars can be used interchangeably.

a low-lift equipment list

hese recipes are pretty low maintenance in the equipment department, and what follows are the items that I recommend having around. A large bowl, sturdy whisk, flexible spatula, baking pans, and measuring tools are a must, but you won't need any electric equipment to make these bakes. I've also included a few of my favorite tools that are very nice to have around if you plan on baking often, which I hope you do!

Baking Pans: You'll need just a few baking pans to make all of the recipes in this book. First up are baking sheets. I recommend having at least two **large baking sheets** that measure about 18 × 13 inches (often sold as "half-sheet pans") that are light-colored aluminum rimmed pans. If you buy high-quality pans (I like Nordic Ware) that have encapsulated galvanized steel rims to prevent warping, they will last just about forever.

It can also be handy to have one or two **baking sheets** measuring 9 × 13 inches (aka a "quarter-sheet pan"), but you won't explicitly need one for any of these recipes. Now, if you don't already own quarter-sheet pans, I am about to change your cooking and baking life. If you are the kind of person who keeps cookie dough balls in the freezer for emergencies (I am this kind of person!), a quarter-sheet pan is the perfect size to bake off a cookie or two.

You'll also need an **8-inch square cake pan.** (If you're a *Snacking Cakes* fan, you'll know this pan already!) I prefer to bake cakes in light-colored metal pans like the natural aluminum pans made by Nordic Ware or aluminized steel pans from USA Pan. The food stylist in me prefers the super straight sides, square corners, and nonstick surface of those made by USA Pan, but both are great choices. They are sturdy, high quality, and should last you a lifetime. Avoid metal baking pans with dark coatings as well as glass or ceramic pans. A 9-inch round pan can be substituted for an 8 × 8-inch square in the cake recipes, but I prefer to bake the bars in a square pan for ease of slicing, and for the tasty edges.

Looking to add to your baking pan library? Here are the sizes and shapes I find most useful in addition to the essentials already mentioned. I recommend light-colored metal baking pans over glass or ceramic for these, too.

- **9 × 5 × 3-inch loaf pan** to turn an 8 × 8-inch cake into a loaf. Add 10 to 20 minutes to the bake time.

- **9 × 13-inch baking pan** for a double batch of cake or bars. Add 5 to 15 minutes to the bake time.

- **10- to 15-cup Bundt pan** for a big beautiful double batch of cake. Add 15 to 30 minutes to the bake time.

- **Standard muffin tin** to turn a cake into muffins or cupcakes. The cake recipes will make about 18 cupcakes and will take 12 to 18 minutes to bake.

Cookie Scoops: Cookie scoops will absolutely change your cookie-baking life. They make it so easy to portion cookie dough into uniform-size cookies. My personal favorite size is a #40 scoop, which measures 1½-tablespoon portions. I prefer the ones that have a thumb trigger—sometimes called "dishers" and sold at restaurant supply stores—rather than ones you have to squeeze with your whole hand. I find that they are much sturdier and longer lasting (I have broken a lot of subpar cookie scoops in my day), but use whatever is comfortable for you. You can find dishers online at webstaurantstore.com or Amazon if you don't have a restaurant supply store in your area. It's also handy to have a slightly smaller scoop and a slightly larger scoop so you can make different size cookies. If you don't have cookie scoops, use a rounded tablespoon measure for these recipes.

Cooling Rack: A wire cooling rack or two is handy to have around to protect your counters from hot pans, but more important, it allows air to circulate around the pans, cutting down on the time you have to wait before digging in to your treats.

Fine-Mesh Sieve: A fine-mesh sieve is great for everything from getting the lumps out of cocoa powder and powdered sugar to rinsing grains and veggies and draining pasta. I am partial to the inexpensive ones you can find at a restaurant supply store.

Measuring Tools: Measuring spoons and a scale are my preferred tools for measuring ingredients. A scale is super accurate and also saves you lots of cleanup. Just think of all of those measuring cups you won't have to wash! I have an OXO digital scale with a pull-out display that I use almost every day. It's a bit of an investment, but if you are serious about baking and cooking, it is a very worthy splurge. If you are as passionate about your measuring cups as I am about my scale, though, I won't stop you. Both weight and volume measurements are provided in my recipes.

Microplane: A handheld zester like a Microplane is useful for finely grating everything from citrus fruit zest and fresh ginger to chocolate.

Mini Offset Spatula: I use a mini offset to loosen the sides of cakes while they are in the pan, scoot cookies around a sheet pan, flip things in a skillet, and more. What I'm saying is that you won't regret spending $5 or less on one, and you'll use it all of the time. I like the 4½-inch spatulas made by Ateco.

Mixing Bowls: The perfect size for a batch of cookies or a snacking cake is 4 quarts. I like stainless steel bowls because they are light, unbreakable, and stack easily, but glass and ceramic are great, too. Something a little smaller will be just fine for a batch of glaze or frosting, but honestly, I usually just wash out my batter bowl and use it again for the glaze. No need to get two things out of the cabinet!

Oven Thermometer: If you are a frequent baker, an oven thermometer is one of the very best gifts you can give yourself. Ovens, especially older models, can be off by enough degrees to make baking very frustrating. It's worth picking one up for a few dollars the next time you go to the kitchen shop.

Parchment Paper: I keep a big box of precut 16 × 12-inch parchment sheets rather than a roll on hand and use them constantly, but both work just fine. If you keep sheets around, they'll fit perfectly on a half-sheet pan and you can cut them in half to make a little parchment sling for an 8 × 8-inch pan or 9 × 5 × 3-inch loaf pan.

Silicone Spatula: A sturdy, but flexible spatula will help ensure your batters are evenly mixed and your bowls are scraped clean. I am partial to the spatulas made by GIR and Le Creuset.

Whisk: A 10-inch metal balloon whisk is going to be your best friend. Make sure it's sturdy and has a comfortable handle. OXO makes a great one that I highly recommend.

How to Make a Parchment Sling

PARCHMENT LINING INSTRUCTIONS:
Cut a length of parchment paper the width of the inside of your baking pan and long enough to come up two of the sides. If the pan is not square, make sure the overhang comes up the two longer sides of the pan.

Brush the inside of the pan with butter or spray with pan spray.

Lay the parchment paper inside of the pan and smooth it against the bottom and sides.

When your bake is cool enough to handle, use the parchment paper to lift it out of the pan.

how to store your bakes

cookies

Chewy, glazed, and frosted cookies will last for about 4 days on the counter, and crisp cookies and shortbread will last even longer, but all are best enjoyed within the first 2 to 3 days. There are a few ways around this:

1. Eat all of the cookies right away.

2. Bake all of the cookies, and by the next day store any leftovers in a freezer bag or an airtight container in the freezer for up to 2 months. Thaw them at room temperature for a few minutes before eating.

3. Do a little prep work so you can have fresh cookies now and fresh cookies later (see box, opposite).

bars

Baked and sliced bars keep well in the freezer in an airtight container for up to 2 months. Separate the layers of bars with sheets of parchment paper. Thaw them at room temperature for a few minutes before eating, or just eat them frozen. I admit, I love a frozen brownie from time to time.

cakes, quick breads, and muffins

Cakes and quick breads keep well, covered, at room temperature for 3 to 4 days. I'm sure you'll find yourself sneaking a little slice of cake every time you walk by until somehow, magically, the cake is just . . . gone? Cakes made with fresh fruit or cream cheese should be stored in the fridge after a day or two. Cakes and quick breads also freeze very well if they are carefully wrapped. They will keep for about 1 month in the freezer. Thaw at room temperature before eating.

Muffins are best in the first 2 days after baking, but they also freeze exceptionally well for about 2 months if they are carefully wrapped. Warm them gently in a toaster oven, or even better, slice them in half, butter the cut sides, and toast them in a pan.

fresh cookies now, fresh cookies later

In my opinion, some cookies are just a little better warm from the oven, especially chocolatey ones, so sometimes I bake a few cookies the moment I make the dough and save some of the dough to bake later. This technique works best with cookies like New Favorite Chocolate Chip Cookies (page 61), White Chocolate Macadamia Nut Cookies (page 74), and Chocolate Peanut Butter Brownie Cookies (page 36), rather than thin and crispy cookies or cookies that are baked and then glazed.

To save some cookies for later, portion out all of the cookie dough onto the baking sheets. Bake off what you'd like to have now. (If you are baking only one sheet of cookies, reduce the baking time called for in the recipe by 1 or 2 minutes.) Refrigerate or freeze the remaining dough on the sheets until firm. Once firm, place the dough balls in a freezer bag or airtight container and freeze for up to 2 months.

Bake the dough balls from frozen, according to the recipe. Note that they will take 1 or 2 minutes longer to bake and will spread less than if they were baked from room-temperature dough. Cookies made from frozen dough will also have a deeper, fuller flavor, especially cookies made with brown butter.

cookies

Everyone loves a cookie, and this chapter covers it all. There are chewy ooey-gooey cookies, thin crisp ones, and perfectly tender shortbread. We'll also cover lots of flavors, from bright and fruity to toasty and spicy to chocolatey, and my favorite, sweet and salty. All of these recipes make about twenty cookies give or take a few and you can bake them all right away, no dough chilling or multiple batches necessary.

Chocolate Peanut Butter Brownie Cookies

MAKES 18 COOKIES

During my sophomore year of college, my brother lived one town over, and some weekends I'd head over to his apartment to hang and cook. I baked many batches of these perfectly sweet-salty little bites, and I'd take the extras to share with my dormmates for a little respite from the less than stellar cuisine at the dining hall. I started by making the recipe on the back of the peanut butter chip bag, but I've updated it here to make it a little less sweet and a little more chocolatey and chewy. Feel free to add some chocolate chips into the mix to make it even *more* chocolatey.

8 tablespoons (113g)
unsalted butter, melted

¾ cup (150g) granulated sugar

1 large egg, cold from the fridge

1 tablespoon neutral oil

1 teaspoon vanilla extract

½ teaspoon fine sea salt

½ cup (45g) Dutch process
cocoa powder, sifted if lumpy

½ teaspoon baking powder

¾ cup plus 2 tablespoons (112g)
all-purpose flour

¾ cup (128g) peanut butter chips

Flaky sea salt

1. Position two racks as close to the center of the oven as possible and preheat to 350°F. Line two large, rimmed baking sheets with parchment paper.

2. In a large bowl, combine the melted butter and sugar and whisk until well combined, about 30 seconds.

3. Add the egg, oil, vanilla, and fine sea salt and whisk until smooth, thick, and glossy, about 30 seconds.

4. Whisk in the cocoa powder until smooth. Whisk in the baking powder. Fold in the flour and peanut butter chips with a spatula. Mix until no streaks of flour remain and the chips are evenly distributed in the batter.

5. Use a 1½-tablespoon cookie scoop or heaping tablespoon to portion the dough into 18 cookies, 9 on each prepared baking sheet. Sprinkle with flaky sea salt.

6. Bake the cookies until just set and a few cracks appear on top, 9 to 11 minutes, switching racks and rotating the pans front to back halfway through baking. You want them to be soft and fudgy.

7. Let the cookies cool on the baking sheets. Store in an airtight container at room temperature for up to 4 days.

Flavor Variations

ROCKY ROAD BROWNIE COOKIES: Omit the peanut butter chips and fold ⅓ cup (35g) chopped toasted walnuts, ⅓ cup (57g) chocolate chips, and ½ cup (28g) mini marshmallows into the dough. Sprinkle the cookies with flaky sea salt.

SUPER CHOCOLATE BROWNIE COOKIES: Omit the peanut butter chips and fold ¾ cup (128g) milk chocolate, semisweet, or bittersweet chocolate chips into the dough. Sprinkle the cookies with flaky sea salt.

S'MORES BROWNIE COOKIES: Omit the peanut butter chips and fold ½ cup (25g) crushed graham crackers and ½ cup (25g) mini marshmallows into the dough. Sprinkle the cookies with flaky sea salt.

Thick and Chewy Oatmeal Raisin Cookies

MAKES 22 COOKIES

There is something so comforting about a nubbly oatmeal cookie, scented with a tiny bit of spice and packed with raisins. This version is super soft and chewy thanks to a bit of cornstarch in the dough along with lots of oats and raisins. I love these cookies just shy of totally baked through, but bake them another couple of minutes for a crispier-edged, cakier cookie. You can, of course, substitute chocolate chips for the raisins, but as a raisin lover, I never would!

8 tablespoons (113g) unsalted butter, melted

½ cup (100g) packed light brown sugar

¼ cup (50g) granulated sugar

1 large egg, cold from the fridge

2 tablespoons cornstarch

1 teaspoon vanilla extract

½ teaspoon fine sea salt

½ teaspoon ground cinnamon

¼ teaspoon freshly grated nutmeg

¾ teaspoon baking soda

1¼ cups (160g) all-purpose flour

1 cup (100g) old-fashioned rolled oats

1 cup (145g) raisins

1. Position two racks as close to the center of the oven as possible and preheat to 350°F. Line two large, rimmed baking sheets with parchment paper.

2. In a large bowl, combine the melted butter, brown sugar, and granulated sugar. Whisk until well combined, about 30 seconds.

3. Add the egg, cornstarch, vanilla, salt, cinnamon, and nutmeg and whisk until smooth, thick, and glossy, about 30 seconds.

4. Whisk in the baking soda. Fold in the flour, oats, and raisins with a spatula. Mix until no streaks of flour remain and the raisins are evenly distributed in the dough.

5. Use a 1½-tablespoon cookie scoop or heaping tablespoon to portion the dough into 22 cookies, 11 on each prepared baking sheet.

6. Bake the cookies until just set (they will still be pale), 9 to 11 minutes, switching racks and rotating the pans front to back halfway through baking.

7. Let the cookies cool on the baking sheets. Store in an airtight container at room temperature for up to 4 days.

Flavor Variations

OATMEAL CHOCOLATE CHIP COOKIES: Substitute an equal amount of chocolate chips for the raisins.

BUTTERSCOTCH OATMEAL COOKIES: Substitute an equal amount of butterscotch chips for the raisins.

OATMEAL CHOCOLATE CHERRY COOKIES: Substitute ½ cup (72g) dried cherries and ½ cup (85) bittersweet chocolate chips for the raisins.

Monster Cookies

These are a true family favorite, and the baked cookies freeze exceptionally well. My family's original recipe made about four times as many cookies as this, but I managed to scale it down without losing any of the chewy peanut buttery goodness. And bonus, these are naturally gluten-free!

⅔ cup (133g) packed
light brown sugar

½ cup (125g) creamy conventional
peanut butter (not natural)

6 tablespoons (85g)
unsalted butter, melted

1 large egg, cold from the fridge

1 teaspoon vanilla extract

½ teaspoon fine sea salt

1 tablespoon cornstarch

½ teaspoon baking soda

2 cups (210g) quick-cooking oats
(certified gluten-free, if needed)

½ cup (85g) semisweet
chocolate chips

½ cup (100g) candy-coated
chocolate candies, such as M&M's

1. Position two racks as close to the center of the oven as possible and preheat to 350°F. Line two large, rimmed baking sheets with parchment paper.

2. In a large bowl, combine the brown sugar, peanut butter, and melted butter and whisk until well combined, about 30 seconds.

3. Add the egg, vanilla, and salt and whisk until smooth, thick, and glossy, about 30 seconds.

4. Whisk in the cornstarch and baking soda. Fold in the oats, chocolate chips, and chocolate candies with a spatula and stir until well mixed. The dough will seem a little dry and crumbly, but don't worry.

5. Use a 1½-tablespoon cookie scoop or heaping tablespoon to portion the dough into 24 cookies, 12 on each prepared baking sheet. Press the dough tightly in the scoop or use your hands to press each ball together tightly.

6. Bake the cookies until set and light golden, 12 to 14 minutes, switching racks and rotating the pans front to back halfway through baking.

7. Let the cookies cool on the baking sheets. Store in an airtight container at room temperature for up to 4 days.

Flavor Variations

PEANUTTY CHOCOLATE MONSTER COOKIES: Fold in ½ cup (60g) chopped salted peanuts along with the oats. If desired, omit the candy-coated chocolates and add ½ cup (85g) extra chocolate chips—a mix of bittersweet or semisweet and milk is nice.

BLUEBERRY PEANUT BUTTER MONSTER COOKIES: Omit the chocolate chips and chocolate candies and add ½ cup (70g) dried blueberries and ½ cup (85g) white chocolate chips.

CHOOSE YOUR OWN ADVENTURE COOKIES: Switch up the mix-ins with chopped candy bars, mini peanut butter cups, or any other flavored chip that you like!

Soft Grapefruit Cookies

These adorable little cookies are cakey with crisp edges when you first make them and soften as they sit. Topped with a zingy glaze, they will last for a few days on the counter, perfect for teatime or really anytime. If you decide not to glaze them, you can coat them in a dusting of powdered sugar.

Soft Grapefruit Cookies

⅓ cup (63g) neutral oil

3 tablespoons (42g) unsalted butter, melted

½ cup (50g) powdered sugar

¼ cup (50g) granulated sugar

2 teaspoons grated grapefruit zest

1 tablespoon grapefruit juice

¼ teaspoon fine sea salt

1 large egg, cold from the fridge

½ teaspoon baking soda

1¼ cups plus 2 tablespoons (175g) all-purpose flour

Grapefruit Glaze

1½ cups (150g) powdered sugar

2 to 3 tablespoons grapefruit juice

Pinch of salt

Grated grapefruit zest (optional)

1. Position two racks as close to the center of the oven as possible and preheat to 350°F. Line two large, rimmed baking sheets with parchment paper.

2. **MAKE THE COOKIES:** In a large bowl, combine the oil, melted butter, powdered sugar, granulated sugar, grapefruit zest, grapefruit juice, and salt. Whisk until well combined, about 30 seconds. The mixture will appear slightly curdled.

3. Add the egg and whisk until smooth, thick, and glossy, about 30 seconds.

4. Whisk in the baking soda. Fold in the flour with a spatula and mix until no streaks of flour remain.

5. Use a 1½-tablespoon cookie scoop or heaping tablespoon to portion the dough into 16 cookies, 8 on each prepared baking sheet.

6. Bake the cookies until light golden brown, 12 to 14 minutes, switching racks and rotating the pans front to back halfway through baking. Let the cookies cool on the baking sheets.

7. **MEANWHILE, MAKE THE GLAZE:** In a medium bowl, combine the powdered sugar, 2 tablespoons grapefruit juice, and salt. Whisk until smooth, adding a bit more grapefruit juice to make a slow-moving, opaque glaze.

8. Once cooled, dip each cookie into the glaze and place back on the parchment paper. If desired, grate a bit of grapefruit zest directly over the tops. Let the glaze set for a few minutes.

9. Store in an airtight container at room temperature for up to 4 days; the cookies will soften as they sit.

Flavor Variation

GRAPEFRUIT POPPY SEED COOKIES: Add 2 tablespoons poppy seeds to the dough when you fold in the flour.

Malted Sugar Cookies

You are less than thirty minutes away from chewy and perfectly rich sugar cookies. The nutty toastiness of the malted milk powder in this recipe gives these cookies an edge over your average sugar cookies that makes it worth seeking out. Only some of the butter in this recipe is melted, which helps keep the dough cool and thick enough to scoop and bake right away.

8 tablespoons (113g) unsalted butter

1 cup (200g) granulated sugar

1 large egg, cold from the fridge

1 teaspoon vanilla extract

½ teaspoon fine sea salt

¼ teaspoon baking powder

½ teaspoon baking soda

¼ cup (30g) malted milk powder

1½ cups (190g) all-purpose flour

1. Position two racks as close to the center of the oven as possible and preheat to 350°F. Line two large, rimmed baking sheets with parchment paper.

2. On the stovetop or in a microwave, melt 4 tablespoons of the butter. Cut the remaining 4 tablespoons into 8 pieces.

3. In a large bowl, combine the melted butter, butter pieces, and ¾ cup (150g) of the sugar and whisk vigorously until smooth and creamy. The unmelted butter may get stuck in the whisk at first, but just keep going until the mixture is light and pale. A few small lumps of unmelted butter are okay; they will smooth out when you add the egg and vanilla.

4. Add the egg, vanilla, and salt and whisk until thickened and pale, about 45 seconds.

5. Whisk in the baking powder and baking soda. Whisk in the malted milk powder. Fold in the flour with a spatula and mix until no streaks of flour remain. The dough will be soft.

6. Place the remaining ¼ cup (50g) sugar in a shallow bowl. Use a 1½-tablespoon cookie scoop or heaping tablespoon to portion the dough into 20 cookies. Toss each piece of dough in the bowl of sugar as you go. Arrange the cookies evenly on the prepared baking sheets, 10 on each sheet.

7. Bake the cookies until just set and barely golden on the edges, but still quite soft in the center, 8 to 10 minutes, switching racks and rotating the pans front to back halfway through baking.

8. Let the cookies cool on the baking sheets. Store in an airtight container at room temperature for up to 4 days.

Flavor Variation

BERRY MALTED SUGAR COOKIES: Add 2 tablespoons crushed freeze-dried blueberries, raspberries, or strawberries when you add the flour.

Do-It-All Salted Butter Shortbread

MAKES ONE 8 × 8-INCH PAN

This shortbread is rich, buttery, tender, and a perfect balance of sweet and salty. It is also endlessly adaptable, and you'll find lots of flavor variations to follow. You can cut the cookie into neat rectangles or squares, but I like to break it into jagged pieces instead. Bake these low and slow to ensure that they are golden and crisp all of the way through. A shorter bake time will result in a softer, more tender texture; bake them a bit longer for more crispy cookies. If you don't have salted butter around, use unsalted and add an additional ¼ teaspoon salt.

2¼ cups (288g) all-purpose flour

⅔ cup (67g) powdered sugar

½ teaspoon fine sea salt

16 tablespoons (226g) salted butter, melted

1. Position a rack in the center of the oven and preheat to 300°F. Coat an 8 × 8-inch baking pan with cooking spray or brush with butter. Line the pan with two crossed strips of parchment paper that hang over the sides.

2. In a large bowl, combine the flour, powdered sugar, and salt and whisk until smooth and no lumps remain in the sugar.

3. Add the melted butter and stir with a spatula until just combined and no streaks of flour remain.

4. Transfer the shortbread dough to the prepared pan and press it into an even layer with your hands or a flat-bottomed measuring cup.

5. Bake the shortbread until golden brown and crisp, 45 to 55 minutes.

6. Let the shortbread cool in the pan, then use the parchment paper to lift the shortbread out of the pan and cut into squares, or use your hands to break the shortbread into pieces. Store in an airtight container at room temperature for up to 1 week.

Flavor Variations

ROSEMARY CITRUS CACAO NIB SHORTBREAD: Add 2 tablespoons cacao nibs, 1 tablespoon finely chopped rosemary, and 2 teaspoons finely grated orange zest to the flour mixture.

SPICY PARMESAN PEPPER SHORTBREAD: Reduce the powdered sugar to ⅓ cup (33g). Add 1 cup (100g) finely grated parmesan cheese, 1 teaspoon ground black pepper, ½ teaspoon Aleppo pepper (silk chili), and ½ teaspoon ground turmeric to the flour. Sprinkle the dough with some black pepper before baking.

ALMOND POPPY SEED SHORTBREAD: Add 2 tablespoons poppy seeds to the flour mixture. Add 2 teaspoons almond extract along with the melted butter. Sprinkle the dough with 1 tablespoon granulated sugar before baking.

BERRY SHORTBREAD: Finely crush ½ cup (15g) freeze-dried strawberries or raspberries and add them to the flour mixture. Sprinkle the dough with 1 tablespoon granulated sugar before baking.

BUCKWHEAT SHORTBREAD: Substitute 1 cup (128g) buckwheat flour for 1 cup (128g) of the all-purpose flour. Sprinkle the dough with 1 tablespoon granulated sugar before baking.

Thin and Crispy Maple Espresso Cookies

MAKES 16 COOKIES

Slightly bitter espresso and rich maple syrup are a perfect pair in these thin and crisp cookies that highlight two of my favorite morning flavors. They are excellent dipped in a cup of milky coffee or tea and make great ice cream sandwiches, too.

Maple Espresso Cookies

6 tablespoons (85g) unsalted butter, melted

6 tablespoons (75g) granulated sugar

¼ cup (50g) packed light brown sugar

2 tablespoons maple syrup

½ teaspoon ground cinnamon

½ teaspoon fine sea salt

1 large egg, cold from the fridge

½ teaspoon baking soda

1¼ cups plus 2 tablespoons (175g) all-purpose flour

2 teaspoons instant espresso powder

Maple Glaze

1 cup (100g) powdered sugar

3 tablespoons maple syrup

1 to 2 teaspoons water

Pinch of salt

1. Position two racks as close to the center of the oven as possible and preheat to 350°F. Line two large, rimmed baking sheets with parchment paper.

2. **MAKE THE COOKIES:** In a large bowl, combine the melted butter, granulated sugar, brown sugar, maple syrup, cinnamon, and salt. Whisk until smooth and combined, about 30 seconds.

3. Add the egg and whisk until smooth, thick, and glossy.

4. Whisk in the baking soda. Fold in the flour and espresso powder with a spatula. Mix until no streaks of flour remain.

5. Use a 1½-tablespoon cookie scoop or heaping tablespoon to portion the dough into 16 cookies, 8 on each prepared baking sheet.

6. Bake the cookies until golden brown and crisp, 13 to 16 minutes, switching racks and rotating the pans front to back halfway through baking. Let the cookies cool completely on the baking sheets.

7. **MEANWHILE, MAKE THE GLAZE:** In a medium bowl, combine the powdered sugar, maple syrup, 1 teaspoon water, and the salt. Whisk until smooth, adding a bit more water if needed to make a thin but opaque glaze.

8. Once cool, drizzle the cookies with the glaze. Store in an airtight container at room temperature for up to 4 days; the cookies will soften as they sit.

Flavor Variation

THIN AND CRISPY ESPRESSO CHOCOLATE COOKIES: Omit the maple glaze and drizzle the baked and cooled cookies with the cocoa glaze from Extra Chocolatey Prune Cake (page 165).

Blueberry Cornmeal Cookies

MAKES 18 COOKIES

These lemon-scented cookies are chewy, just a bit crunchy from the cornmeal, and super delicious on their own, but the blueberry glaze takes them over the top. To crush the freeze-dried blueberries for the glaze, use a cocktail muddler, the handle of a wooden spoon, or place them in a resealable bag and roll over them with a rolling pin. Just make sure to crush them as finely as possible for the most vibrant purple glaze.

Cornmeal Cookies

1 lemon

10 tablespoons (142g) unsalted butter, melted

¾ cup (150g) granulated sugar

¼ cup (50g) packed light brown sugar

1 large egg, cold from the fridge

½ teaspoon fine sea salt

½ teaspoon baking soda

1½ cups (190g) all-purpose flour

½ cup (65g) fine cornmeal

Blueberry Glaze

2 tablespoons lemon juice, or more as needed

2 cups (200g) powdered sugar

2 tablespoons crushed freeze-dried blueberries

1. Position two racks as close to the center of the oven as possible and preheat to 350°F. Line two large, rimmed baking sheets with parchment paper.

2. **MAKE THE COOKIES:** Zest the lemon into a large bowl, add the melted butter, ½ cup (100g) of the granulated sugar, and the brown sugar and whisk vigorously until smooth, about 30 seconds. Reserve the lemon for the glaze. Add the egg and salt and whisk until combined.

3. Add the baking soda and stir until well combined. Fold in the flour and cornmeal with a spatula. Mix until no streaks of flour remain. The dough will be soft.

4. Place the remaining ¼ cup (50g) granulated sugar in a shallow bowl. Use a 1½-tablespoon cookie scoop or heaping tablespoon to portion the dough, tossing each piece of dough in the bowl of sugar before placing it on the baking sheet. There should be 18 cookies, 9 on each prepared baking sheet.

5. Bake the cookies until set and golden on the edges but still quite soft in the center, 9 to 11 minutes, switching racks and rotating the pans front to back halfway through baking. Let the cookies cool on the baking sheets.

6. **MEANWHILE, MAKE THE GLAZE:** Juice the lemon that you zested for the cookies. Add 2 tablespoons juice, the powdered sugar, and crushed freeze-dried blueberries to a medium bowl. Whisk until smooth. The glaze should be thick but pourable. Add a bit more lemon juice if necessary to make a thick glaze. Let the glaze sit for a few minutes to let the color develop.

7. Once cool, drizzle or spoon the glaze over the cookies. Let the glaze set for a few minutes before serving. Store in an airtight container at room temperature for up to 4 days.

Flavor Variations

STRAWBERRY CORNMEAL COOKIES: Substitute an equal amount of crushed freeze-dried strawberries for the blueberries in the glaze.

RASPBERRY CORNMEAL COOKIES: Substitute an equal amount of crushed freeze-dried raspberries for the blueberries in the glaze.

Coconut Apricot Oat Cookies

MAKES 22 COOKIES

These cookies were inspired by Anzac biscuits, a New Zealand/ Australian treat that was created around the time of the First World War. Now, there are tons of spins on the oaty biscuit. These have a bit of honey in place of the traditional golden syrup, and I've added some apricots and pepitas for fun texture, though they definitely were not in the original. Swap in unsalted non-dairy butter sticks and golden syrup to make these vegan.

8 tablespoons (113g) unsalted butter, melted

¾ cup (150g) packed light brown sugar

¼ cup (75g) mild honey

1 tablespoon water

½ teaspoon baking soda

½ teaspoon ground cinnamon

½ teaspoon fine sea salt

1¼ cups (160g) all-purpose flour

½ cup (50g) old-fashioned rolled oats

½ cup (45g) unsweetened finely shredded coconut

⅓ cup (50g) chopped dried apricots

⅓ cup (50g) pepitas

1. Position two racks as close to the center of the oven as possible and preheat to 350°F. Line two large, rimmed baking sheets with parchment paper.

2. In a large bowl, combine the melted butter, brown sugar, honey, and water and whisk until emulsified, about 30 seconds.

3. Whisk in the baking soda, cinnamon, and salt.

4. Add the flour, oats, coconut, apricots, and pepitas and fold until well combined.

5. Use a 1½-tablespoon cookie scoop or heaping tablespoon to portion the dough into 22 cookies, 11 on each prepared baking sheet.

6. Bake the cookies until golden brown, 14 to 16 minutes, switching racks and rotating the pans front to back halfway through baking.

7. Let the cookies cool completely on the baking sheets. Store in an airtight container at room temperature for up to 1 week.

Flavor Variation

CHERRY WALNUT OAT COOKIES: Substitute an equal amount of chopped dried cherries for the apricots and chopped walnuts for the pepitas. You can also swap in just about any other dried fruit for the apricots and any nut for the pepitas.

Chocolate Chip Crispy Rangers

The cereal in these cookies gives them a light and crispy texture that is so fun to eat. I call for two types of chocolate, but you could just as easily use one or the other or substitute any baking chip or dried fruit that you like! Apricots or cherries would be delicious.

8 tablespoons (113g) unsalted butter, melted

½ cup (100g) packed dark brown sugar

½ cup (100g) granulated sugar

1 large egg, cold from the fridge

2 teaspoons vanilla extract

¾ teaspoon fine sea salt

¾ teaspoon baking powder

½ teaspoon baking soda

1½ cups (190g) all-purpose flour

1½ cups (42g) crispy rice cereal

½ cup (85g) bittersweet chocolate chips

½ cup (85g) milk chocolate chips

Flaky sea salt (optional), for sprinkling

1. Position two racks as close to the center of the oven as possible and preheat to 350°F. Line two large, rimmed baking sheets with parchment paper.

2. In a large bowl, combine the melted butter, brown sugar, and granulated sugar and whisk about 30 seconds. The mixture will be grainy and a bit separated.

3. Add the egg, vanilla, and salt and whisk until smooth, thick, and glossy.

4. Whisk in the baking powder and baking soda. Fold in the flour, cereal, and both chocolate chips with a spatula. Mix until no streaks of flour remain and the cereal and chocolate are evenly distributed in the dough.

5. Use a slightly heaping 1½-tablespoon cookie scoop or heaping tablespoon to portion the dough into 24 cookies, 12 on each prepared baking sheet. If desired, sprinkle with flaky sea salt.

6. Bake the cookies until just set with a few cracks on top, 9 to 11 minutes, switching racks and rotating the pans front to back halfway through baking.

7. Let the cookies cool on the baking sheets. Store in an airtight container at room temperature for up to 4 days.

Flavor Variations

COCONUT CRISPY RANGERS: Reduce the cereal to 1 cup (28g) and add ½ cup (45g) unsweetened finely shredded coconut.

CHERRY CRISPY RANGERS: Reduce the chocolate chips to ½ cup (85g) and add ½ cup (75g) dried cherries.

PEANUT BUTTER CRISPY RANGERS: Reduce the chocolate chips to ½ cup (85g) and add ½ cup (85g) peanut butter chips.

Almond Thumbprints

These barely sweet thumbprints are dairy-, egg-, and gluten-free and they couldn't be easier to throw together. Make sure to use the vegan butter that comes in sticks rather than a tub. For folks who are not avoiding dairy, feel free to substitute an equal amount of melted dairy butter for the vegan butter. This recipe doubles well if you'd like more cookies in your life (who doesn't?). If you have a pastry bag it will make quick work of filling the indents with jam, but a little spoon works, too.

2 cups (200g) almond flour

1 tablespoon cornstarch or tapioca starch

¼ teaspoon fine sea salt

4 tablespoons (56g) unsalted vegan stick butter, melted

¼ cup (70g) maple syrup

1 teaspoon vanilla extract

½ teaspoon almond extract

3 tablespoons smooth jam (apricot and raspberry are my faves)

1. Position a rack in the center of the oven and preheat to 350°F. Line a large, rimmed baking sheet with parchment paper.

2. In a large bowl, combine the almond flour, cornstarch, and salt. Stir until well mixed.

3. Add the melted butter, maple syrup, vanilla, and almond extract. Stir until well combined. The dough will be soft and a bit sticky.

4. Use a 1½-tablespoon cookie scoop or heaping tablespoon to portion the dough into 12 cookies evenly spaced on the prepared baking sheet. They won't spread much so they can be close together. Use the tip of your finger or thumb to press an indent into the center of each dough ball. (You can also use the back of a damp ½-teaspoon measure to make tidy even indents.) Fill each indentation with about ½ teaspoon jam.

5. Bake the cookies until the surface is matte, slightly puffed, and golden at the edges, 10 to 12 minutes.

6. Let the cookies cool on the baking sheet. Store in an airtight container at room temperature or in the fridge for up to 1 week.

Flavor Variations

CHEWY ALMOND POPPY SEED COOKIES: Add 2 teaspoons poppy seeds when you add the melted butter. Add an additional ½ teaspoon of almond extract. Instead of making these thumbprints, use a flat-bottomed glass to gently press the tops of the portioned cookies.

CHOCOLATEY ALMOND THUMBPRINTS: When the cookies come out of the oven, immediately place a chocolate chip or small piece of chopped chocolate on top of the jam in each cookie. The residual heat will melt the chocolate into a delicious puddle.

HAZELNUT THUMBPRINTS: Substitute an equal amount of hazelnut flour for the almond flour. If desired, fill the cookies with chocolate hazelnut spread like Nutella instead of jam.

Malted Chocolate Cookies

MAKES 20 COOKIES

These fudgy and rich chocolate cookies have a bonus ingredient that makes them super special: malted milk powder. The malted milk powder gives these cookies a nutty and toasty depth that complements the chocolate so well. I love these with sweet and creamy milk chocolate, but semisweet or bittersweet works, too. You can also swap in a bit of whole-grain flour to give these an even deeper flavor (I love rye).

8 tablespoons (113g) unsalted butter, melted

¾ cup (150g) granulated sugar

1 large egg, cold from the fridge

1 tablespoon neutral oil

1 teaspoon vanilla extract

½ teaspoon fine sea salt

½ cup (45g) Dutch process cocoa powder, sifted if lumpy

½ teaspoon baking powder

¾ cup (96g) all-purpose flour

¼ cup (30g) malted milk powder

¾ cup (128g) chopped milk chocolate

Flaky sea salt, for sprinkling

1. Position two racks as close to the center of the oven as possible and preheat to 350°F. Line two large, rimmed baking sheets with parchment paper.

2. In a large bowl, combine the melted butter and sugar and whisk until well combined, about 30 seconds.

3. Add the egg, oil, vanilla, and salt and whisk until smooth, thick, and glossy, about 30 seconds.

4. Whisk in the cocoa powder until smooth. Whisk in the baking powder. Fold in the flour and malt powder with a spatula. When a few streaks of flour remain, fold in the chopped milk chocolate and mix until no streaks of flour remain and the chocolate is evenly distributed in the dough.

5. Use a 1½-tablespoon cookie scoop or heaping tablespoon to portion the dough into 20 cookies, 10 on each prepared baking sheet, then sprinkle with flaky sea salt.

6. Bake the cookies until just set with a few cracks on top, 8 to 10 minutes, switching racks and rotating the pans front to back halfway through baking. You want them to be soft and fudgy.

7. Let the cookies cool on the baking sheets. Store in an airtight container at room temperature for up to 4 days.

Flavor Variation

MALTED CHOCOLATE WHOLE-GRAIN COOKIES: Reduce the all-purpose flour to ¼ cup (32g) and add ½ cup (64g) dark rye, light rye, or whole wheat flour.

New Favorite Chocolate Chip Cookies

Listen, I know there are a million recipes out there for chocolate chip cookies. But may I make a case for one more? Between my years in the bakery and as a recipe developer, I've baked thousands, and I've picked up a few preferences along the way. These have the whole-grain goodness of Kim Boyce's version and the melted butter and crisp-chewy texture of Tara O'Brady's, along with some of my own adjustments to make these my ideal chocolate chippers.

10 tablespoons (142g) cold unsalted butter

½ cup plus 2 tablespoons (125g) packed light brown sugar

½ cup (100g) granulated sugar

1 large egg, cold from the fridge

1½ teaspoons vanilla extract

¾ teaspoon fine sea salt

½ teaspoon baking powder

½ teaspoon baking soda

1 cup plus 2 tablespoons (142g) all-purpose flour

½ cup (65g) whole wheat flour

Heaping ½ cup (90g) chopped bittersweet or semisweet chocolate, plus more for topping

Flaky sea salt (optional)

1. Position two racks as close to the center of the oven as possible and preheat to 350°F. Line two large, rimmed baking sheets with parchment paper.

2. Cut the butter into tablespoons. In a small skillet or saucepan with a light-colored interior, melt 8 tablespoons (113g) of the butter over medium heat. Once melted, cook the butter, stirring constantly, until the milk solids are deep golden brown, about 3 minutes.

3. In a large bowl, combine the brown butter and the remaining 2 tablespoons (29g) solid butter. Whisk gently until the butter is melted. Add the brown sugar and granulated sugar and whisk until combined, about 30 seconds. The mixture will be a bit grainy and separated.

4. Add the egg, vanilla, and fine sea salt and whisk until smooth, thick, and glossy.

5. Whisk in the baking powder and baking soda. Fold in the all-purpose flour, whole wheat flour, and chopped chocolate with a spatula. Mix until no streaks of flour remain and the chocolate is evenly distributed in the dough.

6. Use a 1½-tablespoon cookie scoop or heaping tablespoon to portion the dough into 22 cookies, 11 on each prepared baking sheet. Gently press a few pieces of chocolate on the top of each cookie. If desired, sprinkle with flaky sea salt.

7. Bake the cookies until just set with a few cracks on top, 8 to 11 minutes, switching racks and rotating the pans front to back halfway through baking.

8. Let the cookies cool on the baking sheets. Store in an airtight container at room temperature for up to 4 days.

(recipe continues)

Flavor Variation

CHOCOLATE CHIPLESS COOKIES: I know there are people out there who like a chocolate chip cookie, minus the chips, so feel free to leave out the chips and enjoy all of the brown-buttery, brown-sugary goodness without them.

Hot Tip

You can bake them right away or scoop and refrigerate the dough and bake them over the course of a few days. Add a minute or so to the bake time if you are baking the cookies from the refrigerator. These have a moderate amount of chopped bittersweet chocolate, so they are a little less rich than some, but as always, adjust to your own tastes.

Vegan Chocolate Chip Cookies

These cookies come together quickly with pantry staples, so if you avoid dairy and eggs for dietary reasons or if you are just plain out of those ingredients, you can have a delicious chocolate chip cookie. Unrefined coconut oil will impart some coconut flavor, so keep that in mind if you use it instead of a refined coconut oil.

10 tablespoons (125g) liquid coconut oil

½ cup (100g) packed organic dark brown sugar

½ cup (100g) organic cane sugar

3 tablespoons cold water

1½ teaspoons vanilla extract

½ teaspoon fine sea salt

¼ teaspoon baking powder

½ teaspoon baking soda

1 cup (130g) whole wheat flour

¾ cup (96g) all-purpose flour

Heaping ½ cup (90g) chopped vegan chocolate, plus more for topping

Flaky sea salt (optional), for sprinkling

1. Position two racks as close to the center of the oven as possible and preheat to 350°F. Line two large, rimmed baking sheets with parchment paper.

2. In a large bowl, combine the coconut oil, brown sugar, cane sugar, water, vanilla, and fine sea salt and whisk until smooth, about 30 seconds. The mixture will start out separated but will smooth out and come together.

3. Whisk in the baking powder and baking soda. Fold in the whole wheat flour, all-purpose flour, and chopped chocolate with a spatula. Mix until no streaks of flour remain and the chocolate is evenly distributed in the dough.

4. Use a 1½-tablespoon cookie scoop or heaping tablespoon to portion the soft dough into 20 cookies, 10 on each prepared baking sheet. Gently press a few pieces of chocolate on the top of each cookie. If desired, sprinkle with flaky sea salt.

5. Bake the cookies until just set with a few cracks on top, 10 to 13 minutes, switching racks and rotating the pans front to back halfway through baking.

6. Let the cookies cool on the baking sheets. Store in an airtight container at room temperature for up to 4 days.

Flavor Variation

VEGAN BUTTER CHOCOLATE CHUNK COOKIES: Substitute ½ cup (113g) unsalted vegan stick butter (such as Earth Balance or Miyoko's Creamery) for the coconut oil. The cookies may spread a bit more than the coconut oil version.

Gluten-Free Chocolate Chip Cookies

My quest for a truly great and easy gluten-free chocolate chip cookie took me through many, many rounds of testing, but I am so pleased with where these guys landed—crisp, chewy, and gooey when warm from the oven. This recipe calls for a store-bought gluten-free flour blend, and I have made them with King Arthur Measure for Measure, Bob's Red Mill 1 to 1 Baking Flour, and Cup4Cup Multipurpose Flour.

8 tablespoons (113g) unsalted butter, melted

½ cup (100g) packed light brown sugar

½ cup (100g) granulated sugar

1 large egg, cold from the fridge

2 teaspoons vanilla extract

¾ teaspoon fine sea salt

½ teaspoon baking powder

½ teaspoon baking soda

1¾ cups (225g) all-purpose gluten-free flour blend (see Hot Tip)

½ cup (50g) almond flour

¾ cup (128g) chopped bittersweet or semisweet chocolate, plus more for topping

Flaky sea salt (optional), for sprinkling

1. Position two racks as close to the center of the oven as possible and preheat to 375°F. Line two large, rimmed baking sheets with parchment paper.

2. In a large bowl, combine the melted butter, brown sugar, and granulated sugar and whisk until combined, about 30 seconds.

3. Add the egg, vanilla, and salt and whisk until smooth, thick, and glossy.

4. Whisk in the baking powder and baking soda. Fold in the flour, almond flour, and chopped chocolate with a spatula. Mix until no streaks of flour remain and the chocolate is evenly distributed in the dough.

5. Use a 1½-tablespoon cookie scoop or heaping tablespoon to portion the dough into 24 cookies, 12 on each prepared baking sheet. Gently press a few pieces of chocolate on the top of each cookie. If desired, sprinkle with flaky sea salt.

6. Bake the cookies until just set with a few cracks on top, 9 to 11 minutes, switching racks and rotating the pans front to back halfway through baking. The cookies will be pale and soft.

7. Let the cookies cool on the baking sheets. Store in an airtight container at room temperature for up to 4 days.

Hot Tip

If you use the King Arthur blend, add 1 tablespoon water when you add the egg and vanilla. The Cup4Cup cookies bake up a bit flatter than the other two blends, but they all make great cookies.

Thin and Crispy Chocolate Cacao Nib Cookies

I used to say that I didn't like crispy chocolate chip cookies, but when I was introduced to Tate's legendary version I was an instant convert. There is something very satisfying about a crisp and crunchy cookie, and it somehow feels a little less rich than a gooey chewy one, making it perfect for snacking. These have a handful of cacao nibs in addition to the chocolate, which add lovely texture, but you can skip them or replace with chopped toasted nuts if you don't keep nibs in your pantry. These also make excellent ice cream sandwiches.

8 tablespoons (113g)
unsalted butter, melted

½ cup (100g) granulated sugar

¼ cup (50g) packed
dark brown sugar

1 large egg, cold from the fridge

1 teaspoon vanilla extract

½ teaspoon fine sea salt

½ teaspoon baking soda

1 cup plus 1 tablespoon (136g)
all-purpose flour

⅓ cup (56g) finely chopped
bittersweet or semisweet chocolate

2 tablespoons cacao nibs

1. Position two racks as close to the center of the oven as possible and preheat to 350°F. Line two large, rimmed baking sheets with parchment paper.

2. In a large bowl, combine the melted butter, granulated sugar, and brown sugar and whisk until combined, about 30 seconds.

3. Add the egg, vanilla, and salt and whisk until smooth, thick, and glossy.

4. Whisk in the baking soda. Fold in the flour, chopped chocolate, and cacao nibs with a spatula. Mix until no streaks of flour remain and the chocolate and nibs are evenly distributed in the dough.

5. Use a 1½-tablespoon cookie scoop or heaping tablespoon to portion the dough into 18 cookies, 9 on each prepared baking sheet.

6. Bake the cookies until they are golden and crisp, 16 to 20 minutes, switching racks and rotating the pans front to back halfway through baking.

7. Let the cookies cool on the baking sheets. Store in an airtight container at room temperature for up to 4 days.

Flavor Variation

THIN AND CRISPY WALNUT COOKIES: Add ½ cup (55g) finely chopped walnuts in place of, or in addition to, the cacao nibs. This may result in an additional cookie or two depending on how you portion them.

Fudgy Sesame Oat Cookies

These rich and fudgy cookies are cooked in a saucepan, rather than baked in the oven for those days when turning on the oven is not an option. Don't be tempted to use chopped chocolate here; the stabilizers in the chocolate chips help these cookies set. You can also swap the butter and milk for plant-based versions to make these vegan. I like them best made with Miyoko's Creamery butter and oat milk. You can make these little bites any size you like: I like to use my go-to 1½-tablespoon scoop, but smaller bites would be great, too.

1 cup (200g) granulated sugar

6 tablespoons (85g) unsalted butter, cut into tablespoons

⅓ cup (30g) Dutch process cocoa powder, sifted if lumpy

6 tablespoons (85g) milk, any kind

¼ teaspoon fine sea salt

½ cup (125g) tahini, well stirred

1½ cups (158g) quick-cooking oats

½ cup (45g) sliced almonds, toasted

½ cup (85g) bittersweet or semisweet chocolate chips

Flaky sea salt (optional), for sprinkling

Sesame seeds (optional), for sprinkling

1. Line two large, rimmed baking sheets with parchment paper.

2. In a 2-quart saucepan, combine the sugar, butter, cocoa, milk, and salt. Set the pan over medium-high heat and whisk the mixture occasionally until the butter has melted and there are no lumps in the cocoa. Bring to a rolling boil and boil for 1 minute. There should be vigorous bubbles from edge to edge of the pan.

3. Remove from the heat and whisk in the tahini. Stir in the oats and almonds. Stir in the chocolate chips. Some of the chips will melt and that's okay.

4. Use a 1½-tablespoon cookie scoop or heaping tablespoon to portion the dough into 25 cookies, evenly spaced on the prepared baking sheets. These won't spread, so they can be quite close together. If desired, sprinkle with flaky salt and sesame seeds.

5. Let the cookies cool and set for about 20 minutes before eating them. These cookies are soft at room temperature and gloriously fudgy straight from the fridge, where they will last for about 1 week.

Flavor Variation

FUDGY PEANUT BUTTER OAT COOKIES: Substitute an equal amount of peanut butter for the tahini.

Magical Peanut Butter Cookies

These peanut butter cookies are so easy to make, deliciously fudgy, and surprisingly vegan. You can press a fork into the top for that classic crisscross look or you can gently press the tops with a flat-bottomed glass for a super-appealing crackly top. You can even make them thumbprints by baking the dough balls and then pressing a little indent into the center of each warm cookie to fill with jam, dulce de leche, or melted chocolate. Feel free to substitute dairy milk for the nondairy here. If you have only unsalted peanut butter on hand, add another big pinch of salt to the recipe.

1 cup (250g) salted unsweetened natural peanut butter, well stirred

¾ cup (150g) organic light or dark brown sugar

¼ cup (55g) unsweetened nondairy milk, any kind

1 tablespoon neutral oil

2 teaspoons vanilla extract

½ teaspoon fine sea salt

¾ teaspoon baking soda

½ cup (64g) all-purpose flour

1. Position two racks as close to the center of the oven as possible and preheat to 350°F. Line two large, rimmed baking sheets with parchment paper.

2. In a large bowl, combine the peanut butter, brown sugar, milk, oil, vanilla, and salt. Stir vigorously with a spatula until smooth, about 30 seconds.

3. Stir in the baking soda. Fold in the flour with the spatula and mix until no streaks of flour remain.

4. Use a 1½-tablespoon cookie scoop or heaping tablespoon to portion the dough into 18 cookies, 9 on each prepared baking sheet. Use a glass with a flat bottom to gently press down each cookie. (Alternatively, use a fork to press a crisscross pattern into the top of each cookie.)

5. Bake the cookies until set, golden brown on the edges, with a few cracks on top, 11 to 13 minutes, switching racks and rotating the pans front to back halfway through baking.

6. Let the cookies cool on the baking sheets. Store in an airtight container at room temperature for up to 4 days.

Flavor Variations

PEANUT BUTTER THUMBPRINTS: Bake the cookies without pressing them down before baking. When they are just out of the oven, carefully use a ½-teaspoon measure to gently press an indent in the center of each cookie. Fill the indent with your favorite jam, dulce de leche, or a few pieces of chopped chocolate topped with flaky sea salt.

EXTRA PEANUTTY COOKIES: Roll the unbaked dough balls in ½ cup (55g) finely chopped salted roasted peanuts mixed with 1 tablespoon granulated or turbinado sugar. Press the cookies gently with a flat-bottomed glass before baking.

White Chocolate Macadamia Nut Cookies

MAKES 22 COOKIES

Like many children in the '90s, I spent a lot of time in shopping malls with the scent from Mrs. Fields cookies beckoning me to stop. I always went for the white chocolate macadamia nut cookie, which seemed fancier than the rest of the bunch. When I first started baking at home, my mom bought me the *Mrs. Fields Cookie Book* from TJ Maxx and I'm pretty sure I baked every single recipe. These are my homage to those afternoons in the mall, and Mrs. Fields who is not shy with the vanilla extract. If you can find it, caramelized white chocolate like Valrhona Dulcey is delicious in these.

10 tablespoons (142g) cold unsalted butter, cut into tablespoons

1 cup (200g) packed light brown sugar

1 large egg, cold from the fridge

2 teaspoons vanilla extract

¾ teaspoon fine sea salt

½ teaspoon baking powder

½ teaspoon baking soda

1⅓ cups (170g) all-purpose flour

¾ cup (100g) chopped salted macadamia nuts

½ cup (85g) white chocolate chips or chopped white chocolate

Flaky sea salt (optional), for sprinkling

1. Position two racks as close to the center of the oven as possible and preheat to 350°F. Line two large, rimmed baking sheets with parchment paper.

2. In a small skillet or saucepan with a light-colored interior, melt 8 tablespoons (113g) of the butter over medium heat. Once melted, cook the butter, stirring constantly, until the milk solids are deep golden brown, about 3 minutes.

3. In a large bowl, combine the brown butter, the remaining 2 tablespoons (29g) cold butter, and the brown sugar. Whisk until combined and the butter melts, about 1 minute. The mixture will be a bit grainy and separated.

4. Add the egg, vanilla, and salt and whisk until smooth, thick, and glossy, about 30 seconds.

5. Whisk in the baking powder and baking soda. Fold in the flour with a spatula and when a few streaks of flour remain, add the nuts and white chocolate. Mix until no streaks of flour remain and the chocolate and nuts are evenly distributed in the dough.

6. Use a 1½-tablespoon cookie scoop or heaping tablespoon to portion the dough into 22 cookies, 11 on each prepared baking sheet. If desired, sprinkle with flaky sea salt.

7. Bake the cookies until just set with a few cracks on top, 9 to 11 minutes, switching racks and rotating the pans front to back halfway through baking.

8. Let the cookies cool on the baking sheets. Store in an airtight container at room temperature for up to 4 days.

Flavor Variations

DARK CHOCOLATE MACADAMIA NUT COOKIES: Substitute an equal amount of dark chocolate for the white.

WHITE CHOCOLATE PECAN COOKIES: Substitute an equal amount of chopped toasted pecans for the macadamia nuts.

Banana Brownie Cookies

These fudgy chocolate banana cookies are pantry heroes, and a great use for that single brown banana you probably have on the counter right now. You don't even need any butter or eggs to make them. They are perfect alongside a cold glass of milk, and they also make excellent ice cream sandwiches, if you are in the mood for dessert.

½ cup (125g) mashed very ripe banana (about 1 banana)

⅓ cup (63g) neutral oil

¾ cup (150g) organic cane sugar

½ teaspoon fine sea salt

½ teaspoon baking powder

½ teaspoon baking soda

⅓ cup (30g) Dutch process cocoa powder, sifted if lumpy

1 cup (128g) all-purpose flour

½ cup (55g) chopped toasted pecans or walnuts

½ cup (85g) bittersweet vegan chocolate chips

1. Position two racks as close to the center of the oven as possible and preheat to 350°F. Line two large, rimmed baking sheets with parchment paper.

2. In a large bowl, combine the banana, oil, sugar, and salt and whisk until well combined, about 30 seconds.

3. Add the baking powder, baking soda, and cocoa powder and whisk again until smooth. Fold in the flour, pecans, and chocolate chips with a spatula. Mix until no streaks of flour remain.

4. Use a 1½-tablespoon cookie scoop or heaping tablespoon to portion the dough into 20 cookies, 10 on each prepared baking sheet.

5. Bake the cookies until set with a few cracks on top, 14 to 17 minutes, switching racks and rotating the pans front to back halfway through baking.

6. Let the cookies cool on the baking sheets. Store in an airtight container at room temperature for up to 4 days.

Flavor Variation

EXTRA NUTTY BANANA BROWNIE COOKIES: Substitute an equal amount of toasted pecans or walnuts for the chocolate chips.

Salt and Pepper Olive Oil Shortbread

MAKES ONE 8 × 8-INCH PAN

I love a sweet and savory baked good, and this shortbread comes together faster than it will take for your oven to heat. It is made with olive oil rather than butter, so it is super pantry friendly as well. You can cut the cookie into neat rectangles or squares, but I sometimes like to break it into jagged pieces.

2 cups (256g) all-purpose flour

⅔ cup (67g) powdered sugar

1 teaspoon freshly ground black pepper, plus more for sprinkling

¾ teaspoon fine sea salt

¾ cup (143g) mild-tasting olive oil

1 tablespoon granulated sugar, for sprinkling

¼ teaspoon flaky sea salt, for sprinkling

1. Position a rack in the center of the oven and preheat to 350°F. Coat an 8 × 8-inch baking pan with cooking spray or brush with oil. Line the pan with two crossed strips of parchment paper that hang over the sides.

2. In a large bowl, combine the flour, powdered sugar, pepper, and fine sea salt until smooth, stirring until no lumps remain in the sugar.

3. Add the oil and stir with a spatula until just combined.

4. Transfer the shortbread dough to the prepared pan and press it into an even layer with your hands or a flat-bottomed measuring cup. Top with the granulated sugar, a sprinkling of black pepper, and the flaky salt.

5. Bake the shortbread until golden brown and crisp, 30 to 35 minutes.

6. Let the shortbread cool in the pan set on a rack, then use the parchment paper to lift the shortbread out of the pan and cut into pieces or use your hands to break the shortbread into pieces. Store in an airtight container at room temperature for up to 1 week.

Flavor Variations

HERBED OLIVE OIL SHORTBREAD: Add about 2 tablespoons finely chopped woody herbs, such as thyme, rosemary, or sage, to the flour mixture.

WALNUT OLIVE OIL SHORTBREAD: Add ½ cup (55g) finely chopped toasted walnuts to the flour mixture.

CITRUS OLIVE OIL SHORTBREAD: Omit the pepper and add about 1 tablespoon finely grated lemon or orange zest when you add the olive oil.

Snack Attacks

MAKES 24 COOKIES

Before Milk Bar was an international brand, it was a little storefront attached to the restaurant Momofuku Noodle Bar in New York's East Village. I would pop in to that cozy space on East 13th Street and marvel at how unbelievably good it smelled. I was a baker in a restaurant at the time, but I always dreamed of working at Milk Bar. These are inspired by their famous compost cookies but with a few tweaks. I've used brown butter and dark brown sugar, and my combo of mix-ins includes some crushed buttery Ritz crackers, which give these cookies a toothsome texture that is just irresistible. Use thin and crispy potato chips here over thicker, kettle-cooked types; a snack-size bag is the perfect amount. I've been tempted to crush up a handful of Oreos and throw them in there, too. These are super flexible, though, so use whatever sweet and salty mix-ins you have on hand, with even more ideas following (see Kitchen Sink Cookies, opposite).

10 tablespoons (142g) cold unsalted butter, cut into tablespoons

¾ cup (150g) packed dark brown sugar

¼ cup (50g) granulated sugar

1 large egg, cold from the fridge

2 teaspoons vanilla extract

½ teaspoon fine sea salt

½ teaspoon baking powder

½ teaspoon baking soda

1½ cups plus 2 tablespoons (208g) all-purpose flour

⅔ cup (28g) crushed potato chips, such as Lay's

½ cup (25g) crushed Ritz crackers (about 8 crackers)

⅓ cup (57g) chopped bittersweet chocolate or chips

¼ cup (43g) butterscotch chips

1. Position two racks as close to the center of the oven as possible and preheat to 350°F. Line two large, rimmed baking sheets with parchment paper.

2. In a small skillet or saucepan with a light-colored interior, melt 8 tablespoons (113g) of the butter over medium heat. Once melted, cook the butter, stirring constantly, until the milk solids are deep golden brown, about 3 minutes.

3. Pour the brown butter into a large bowl and add the remaining 2 tablespoons (29g) solid butter, the brown sugar, and granulated sugar. Whisk until the butter melts, about 30 seconds. The mixture will be a little bit separated.

4. Add the egg, vanilla, and salt and whisk until smooth, thick, and glossy.

5. Add the baking powder and baking soda and stir until well combined. Fold in the flour with a spatula, and when there are a few streaks of flour remaining, add the potato chips, crackers, chopped chocolate, and butterscotch chips. Keep stirring until no streaks of flour remain and the mix-ins are evenly distributed.

6. Use a 1½-tablespoon cookie scoop or heaping tablespoon to portion the dough into 24 cookies, 12 on each prepared baking sheet.

7. Bake the cookies until just set with a few cracks on top, but still quite soft in the center, 9 to 11 minutes, switching racks and rotating the pans front to back halfway through baking.

8. Let the cookies cool on the baking sheets. Store in an airtight container at room temperature for up to 4 days.

Flavor Variation

KITCHEN SINK COOKIES: Substitute pretzels or cornflakes for either of the salty mix-ins or substitute any other type of chips you have on hand for chocolate and butterscotch chips. The sky's (your pantry's) the limit!

bars, brownies, and bark

Bars and brownies are some of my very favorite things to bake. They are quick and easy, and dare I say, a little lazy. All of the beauty of a cookie with no scooping necessary, because sometimes even that is a step too far in pursuit of a snack. They also lend themselves well to just about any flavor you can imagine, from rich and fudgy to fruity and citrusy. You'll also find a few recipes for cookie bark, a giant crunchy cookie that you bake on a sheet pan and then break up into whatever size pieces suits your mood.

Chewy Cocoa Brownies

Everyone needs a back-pocket brownie recipe, and this is mine. It hits that sweet spot of chewy, fudgy, and just the tiniest bit cakey. Browning the butter gives these brownies a wonderful deep flavor. Plus, when you combine the hot butter with the sugar, it melts the sugar a bit and gives these brownies a gorgeous crinkly top. I know ⅛ teaspoon baking soda seems a fiddly quantity, but it gives these brownies just the right amount of lift. Trust me, I tried them every different way. If you prefer a fudgier brownie, you can leave it out entirely.

10 tablespoons (142g) cold unsalted butter, cut into tablespoons

1 cup plus 2 tablespoons (225g) granulated sugar

¼ cup (48g) neutral oil

1 teaspoon vanilla extract

½ teaspoon fine sea salt

2 large eggs, cold from the fridge

⅛ teaspoon baking soda

⅔ cup (60g) Dutch process cocoa powder, sifted if lumpy

½ cup (64g) all-purpose flour

½ cup (85g) chopped chocolate or chocolate chips, any kind you like

1. Position a rack in the center of the oven and preheat to 350°F. Coat an 8 × 8-inch baking pan with cooking spray or brush with butter. Line the pan with a strip of parchment paper that hangs over two of the sides.

2. In a small skillet or saucepan with a light-colored interior, melt the butter over medium heat. Once melted, cook the butter, stirring constantly until the milk solids are deep golden brown, about 3 minutes.

3. In a large bowl, combine the sugar and the hot brown butter and vigorously whisk for 45 seconds.

4. Add the oil, vanilla, and salt and whisk until combined and emulsified. Whisk in the eggs.

5. Whisk in the baking soda and cocoa powder until just combined. Fold in the flour and chocolate chips with a spatula. Mix until no streaks of flour remain. Don't overmix. Transfer the batter to the prepared pan and smooth the top.

6. Bake the brownies until puffy and set with just a bit of wiggle in the center, 25 to 30 minutes.

7. Let the brownies cool completely in the pan on a rack. Once cool, run a thin knife or offset spatula along the edges of the pan that are not protected by the parchment, and use the parchment paper to lift the brownies out of the pan and slice. Store in an airtight container at room temperature for up to 4 days, or a few days longer in the fridge. These are gloriously fudgy when cold.

Flavor Variation

PEANUT BUTTER BROWNIES: Dollop ½ cup (125g) creamy conventional peanut butter over the brownie batter in the pan and use a knife or skewer to swirl it in a bit.

Frosted Lemon-Lime Sugar Cookie Bars

Chewy sugar cookie bars are a perfect canvas for bright citrusy flavors and would make an excellent cookie cake if that's your thing.

Lemon-Lime Sugar Cookie

1 lemon

1 lime

8 tablespoons (113g) unsalted butter, melted

2 ounces (57g) cream cheese, cut into 4 pieces

1 cup (200g) granulated sugar

1 large egg, cold from the fridge

½ teaspoon fine sea salt

¼ teaspoon baking powder

1½ cups (190g) all-purpose flour

Lemon-Lime Frosting

4 tablespoons (56g) unsalted butter, at room temperature

1½ cups (150g) powdered sugar, sifted if lumpy

1 to 2 teaspoons lemon juice

1 to 2 teaspoons lime juice

Pinch of salt

Grated lemon or lime zest (optional), for garnish

Sprinkles (optional), for garnish

1. Position a rack in the center of the oven and preheat to 350°F. Coat an 8 × 8-inch baking pan with cooking spray or brush with butter. Line the pan with a strip of parchment paper that hangs over two of the sides.

2. **MAKE THE COOKIE:** In a large bowl, zest the lemon and lime and add the melted butter, cream cheese, and sugar. Whisk until combined, thick, and glossy, about 30 seconds. A few small lumps of cream cheese are okay.

3. Add the egg and salt and whisk until smooth, about 20 seconds.

4. Whisk in the baking powder until smooth. Fold in the flour with a spatula until just combined. The dough will be sticky.

5. Transfer the dough to the prepared pan and use an offset spatula or your hands to spread and press the sticky dough evenly into the pan. Use a bit of oil or cooking spray on your spatula or hands if necessary to keep the dough from sticking.

6. Bake the cookie bars until set and light golden brown, 22 to 26 minutes. (Now is a great time to get the butter for the frosting out of the fridge if you haven't already.)

7. Let the cookie bars cool in the pan set on a rack for about 15 minutes. Then use the parchment to lift them out and onto the rack to cool completely before frosting.

8. **MAKE THE FROSTING:** In a large bowl, use a wooden spoon (or an electric mixer if you have one) to beat the softened butter until smooth. Add the powdered sugar, 1 teaspoon of lemon juice, 1 teaspoon of lime juice, and the salt and mix slowly until the sugar is incorporated. Once incorporated, mix a bit faster until smooth and fluffy. Add more lemon and lime juice if necessary to make a smooth and spreadable frosting. This will take a bit of muscle if you are mixing by hand, but it is doable.

(recipe continues)

9. Spread the frosting over the cooled bars. If desired, grate some lemon or lime zest on top. Store in an airtight container at room temperature or in the fridge for up to 4 days.

Flavor Variations

RAINBOW SPRINKLE SUGAR COOKIE BARS: For the cookies, omit the citrus zest from the dough and add 1½ teaspoons vanilla extract or paste when you add the egg. Fold in ¼ cup (45g) rainbow sprinkles (the long cylindrical type, not the round type) into the dough along with the flour. For the frosting, add 1 teaspoon vanilla extract or paste and substitute milk for the citrus juice. Top the cookies with a few more sprinkles.

STRAWBERRY SUGAR COOKIE BARS: For the cookies, omit the citrus zest and add 3 tablespoons crushed freeze-dried strawberries to the dough along with the flour. For the frosting, add 2 teaspoons crushed freeze-dried strawberries and substitute milk for the citrus juice. Top the cookies with a sprinkling of freeze-dried strawberries.

PINK LEMONADE SUGAR COOKIE BARS: For the cookies, add 2 tablespoons crushed freeze-dried strawberries to the dough along with the flour. For the frosting, add 2 teaspoons crushed freeze-dried strawberries. Top the cookies with a sprinkling of freeze-dried strawberries.

Hot Tip

While the cookies are baking and cooling, get the butter for the frosting out of the fridge to soften so you don't have to wait for it later, or skip the frosting all together.

Blueberry Swirl Blondies

These ooey-gooey berry-swirled blondies are gorgeous and oh so tasty. The brown butter adds a base of toasty nuttiness that helps cut the creamy richness of the white chocolate, and the blueberry adds a punch of vibrant flavor. They are super extra delicious if you can find caramelized white chocolate like Valrhona Dulcey.

10 tablespoons (142g) cold unsalted butter, cut into tablespoons

1 cup (200g) packed dark brown sugar

1 large egg, cold from the fridge

2 teaspoons vanilla extract

½ teaspoon fine sea salt

¼ teaspoon ground cinnamon

¼ teaspoon baking powder

¼ teaspoon baking soda

1½ cups (190g) all-purpose flour

½ cup (85g) white chocolate chips or chopped white chocolate

¼ cup (75g) blueberry jam, well stirred

1. Position a rack in the center of the oven and preheat to 350°F. Coat an 8 × 8-inch baking pan with cooking spray or brush with butter. Line the pan with a strip of parchment paper that hangs over two of the sides.

2. In a small skillet or saucepan with a light-colored interior, melt 8 tablespoons (113g) of the butter over medium heat. Once melted, cook the butter, stirring constantly until the milk solids are deep golden brown, about 3 minutes.

3. In a large bowl, combine the brown sugar and remaining 2 tablespoons (29g) cold butter. Pour the brown butter over the top and whisk until combined and the solid butter is melted, about 30 seconds. The mixture will be a little bit grainy and separated.

4. Add the egg, vanilla, salt, and cinnamon and whisk until smooth and glossy.

5. Whisk in the baking powder and baking soda until smooth. Fold in the flour and white chocolate with a spatula. Mix until no streaks of flour remain.

6. Transfer the batter to the prepared pan and smooth the top. Dollop heaping teaspoons of jam over the top of the batter and then use a skewer or thin knife to swirl the jam into the batter.

7. Bake until golden brown all over and just a bit wiggly in the center, 25 to 27 minutes.

8. Let the blondies cool in the pan on a rack. Once cool, use the parchment paper to lift the bars out of the pan. Store in an airtight container at room temperature for up to 4 days.

Flavor Variation

RED BERRY SWIRL BLONDIES: Stir a bit of grated orange zest into the brown sugar before adding the butter. Substitute milk chocolate or semisweet chocolate for the white chocolate. Substitute strawberry or raspberry jam for the blueberry.

Strawberry Chocolate Almond Butter Bars

MAKES ONE 8 × 8-INCH PAN

Almond butter is pretty mild in flavor, but crisp almonds, chocolate, and punchy freeze-dried strawberries make these a special little snack. Feel free to substitute peanut butter or any other nut butter for the almond butter. If your almond butter is unsalted, add an additional pinch of salt to the dough. Toast the almonds in the oven while the bars are baking to save yourself some prep time.

8 tablespoons (113g) unsalted butter, melted

½ cup (125g) salted natural almond butter, well stirred

1 cup (200g) packed light brown sugar

1 large egg, cold from the fridge

1 teaspoon vanilla extract

½ teaspoon almond extract (optional)

½ teaspoon fine sea salt

½ teaspoon ground cinnamon

¼ teaspoon baking powder

¼ teaspoon baking soda

1 cup (128g) all-purpose flour

¾ cup (128g) semisweet or bittersweet chocolate chips

½ cup (55g) toasted sliced almonds

2 tablespoons crumbled freeze-dried strawberries

Flaky sea salt, for sprinkling

1. Position a rack in the center of the oven and preheat to 350°F. Coat an 8 × 8-inch baking pan with cooking spray or brush with butter. Line the pan with a strip of parchment paper that hangs over two of the sides.

2. In a large bowl, whisk the butter, almond butter, and brown sugar until well combined, about 30 seconds.

3. Add the egg, vanilla, almond extract (if using), fine sea salt, and cinnamon and whisk until smooth and glossy.

4. Whisk in the baking powder and baking soda. Fold in the flour with a spatula and mix until just combined and no streaks of flour remain.

5. Transfer the dough to the prepared pan and use an offset spatula or your hands to press the sticky dough evenly into the pan. Use a bit of oil or cooking spray on your hands if necessary to keep the dough from sticking.

6. Bake until golden brown and just slightly firm, 23 to 28 minutes. Set the pan on a rack and immediately sprinkle the chocolate chips over the top of the bars. Let it sit for 5 minutes without touching; the bars will deflate a bit and the chocolate will melt.

7. Use a spoon or offset spatula to gently and carefully spread the chocolate over the top (the pan will be hot). Sprinkle the almonds and strawberries over the chocolate followed by a sprinkling of flaky salt, then press gently to adhere.

8. Let the bars sit until the pan is cool enough to handle, about 15 minutes, then transfer the pan to the refrigerator to chill until the chocolate is firm, about 20 minutes, before slicing. Store in an airtight container at room temperature for up to 4 days or longer in the fridge.

Flavor Variations

CHOCOLATEY PEANUT BUTTER BARS:
Substitute an equal amount of peanut
butter for the almond butter and
chopped roasted, salted peanuts for the
sliced almonds. Omit the freeze-dried
strawberries.

**RASPBERRY CHOCOLATE ALMOND BUTTER
BARS:** Substitute an equal amount of
crushed freeze-dried raspberries for the
strawberries.

Brown Butter Chocolate Chip Cookie Bark

MAKES ONE 10-ISH-INCH COOKIE

This is a giant crunchy chocolate chip cookie for lazy people (like me!). It's perfect for those times when you want a sweet chocolate chippy treat but can't be bothered to scoop cookies. If you are having people over, you even could whip this up while your guests are around without much fuss. Serve cookie shards with a scoop of ice cream for a super-quick and satisfying dessert.

9 tablespoons (127g) cold unsalted butter, cut into tablespoons

⅓ cup (67g) granulated sugar

⅓ cup (67g) packed light brown sugar

2 teaspoons vanilla extract

¾ teaspoon fine sea salt

½ teaspoon baking soda

1 cup (128g) all-purpose flour

½ cup (65g) semisweet or bittersweet chocolate chips

1. Position a rack in the center of the oven and preheat to 350°F. Line a large, rimmed baking sheet with parchment paper.

2. In a small skillet or saucepan with a light-colored interior, melt 6 tablespoons (85g) of the butter over medium heat. Once melted, cook the butter, stirring constantly until the milk solids are deep golden brown, about 3 minutes.

3. Transfer the brown butter to a large bowl, then add the remaining 3 tablespoons (42g) cold butter and stir until melted. Add the granulated sugar and brown sugar and whisk until well combined, about 30 seconds.

4. Add the vanilla and salt and whisk until smooth.

5. Whisk in the baking soda. Fold in the flour with a spatula and mix until there are a few streaks of flour remaining. Fold in the chocolate chips and keep stirring until no streaks of flour remain and the chocolate is evenly distributed.

6. Transfer the mixture to the prepared pan and press the dough into a thin even round, about the thickness of the chocolate chips. You should have a roughly 10-inch round cookie, but it doesn't need to be perfect. If the mixture is crumbly around the edges, use your fingertips to press the edges together.

7. Bake until golden brown, crisp, and firm to the touch, 17 to 20 minutes.

8. Let cool completely on the pan, then use your hands to break the bark into pieces. Store in an airtight container at room temperature for up to 4 days.

Flavor Variations

NUTTY CRUNCHY CHOCOLATE CHIP COOKIE BARK: Add up to ½ cup (55g) chopped toasted nuts when you add the chocolate chips. Sprinkle flaky sea salt and turbinado sugar on top just before baking.

ESPRESSO CHOCOLATE CHIP COOKIE BARK: Add 1 teaspoon instant espresso powder when you add the vanilla and salt.

Glazed Cookie Butter Bars

If you've never had cookie butter, know that it's made from crushed up speculoos or Biscoff cookies. Maybe you've had them on an airplane? Either way, the warmly spiced cookie butter, combined with buttery rum glaze, gives these bars a cozy holiday vibe. Cookie butter can be found at many large supermarkets and at Trader Joe's, and is easily available online in a pinch.

Cookie Butter Bars

8 tablespoons (113g) unsalted butter, melted

½ cup (125g) speculoos cookie butter

¾ cup (150g) packed light brown sugar

1 large egg, cold from the fridge

1 teaspoon ground cinnamon

½ teaspoon fine sea salt

¼ teaspoon baking powder

¼ teaspoon baking soda

1 cup (128g) all-purpose flour

Butter Rum Glaze

¾ cup (75g) powdered sugar

1 tablespoon dark rum

1 tablespoon (14g) butter, melted

Pinch of ground cinnamon

Pinch of salt

Water, as needed

1. Position a rack in the center of the oven and preheat to 350°F. Coat an 8 × 8-inch baking pan with cooking spray or brush with butter. Line the pan with a strip of parchment paper that hangs over two of the sides.

2. **MAKE THE BARS:** In a large bowl, combine the melted butter, cookie butter, and brown sugar. Whisk until the mixture comes together, then changes to the consistency of Play-Doh, about 1 minute.

3. Add the egg, cinnamon, and salt and whisk until smooth and glossy.

4. Whisk in the baking powder and baking soda. Fold in the flour with a spatula and mix until just combined and no streaks of flour remain.

5. Transfer the dough to the prepared pan and use an offset spatula or your hands to spread the sticky dough evenly into the pan. Use a bit of oil or cooking spray on your hands if necessary to keep the dough from sticking.

6. Bake the bars until golden brown, cracked at the edges, and just slightly firm, 25 to 30 minutes.

7. Let the bars cool slightly in the pan on a rack.

8. **MEANWHILE, MAKE THE GLAZE:** When the bars are just slightly warm, in a medium bowl, whisk together the powdered sugar, rum, melted butter, cinnamon, and salt. Add a bit of water if necessary to make a thick but pourable consistency.

9. Use the parchment paper to lift the bars out of the pan and then pour the glaze over the bars. Spread the glaze evenly over the top. It will be a thin layer. Let the glaze set for a few minutes before slicing. Store in an airtight container at room temperature for up to 4 days.

Flavor Variations

COFFEE COOKIE BUTTER BARS: Omit the butter rum glaze and top the cooled bars with the coffee glaze from Coffee-Glazed Molasses Bars (page 112).

SPICED PEANUT BUTTER COOKIE BARS: Substitute an equal amount of conventional peanut butter for the cookie butter. Add ½ teaspoon ground ginger and ½ teaspoon freshly grated nutmeg when you add the egg, cinnamon, and salt.

Pink Cookie Bars

The first stop on my coffee cart treat quest (second stop, Raspberry Mazurkas, page 108) is the elusive Pink Cookie. Uncle Seth's Pink Cookies are palm-size cookies scented with cardamom and topped with a pink-tinted cream cheese and almond frosting. Here, I've made them into a pat-in-the pan cookie bar with a layer of perfectly pink cream cheese frosting scented with a bit of almond extract.

Cookie Bars

1¾ cups (225g) all-purpose flour

½ cup (100g) granulated sugar

½ teaspoon ground cardamom

½ teaspoon baking powder

½ teaspoon fine sea salt

12 tablespoons (170g) unsalted butter, melted

1 teaspoon almond extract

1 teaspoon vanilla extract

Cream Cheese Frosting

2 tablespoons (29g) unsalted butter, at room temperature

2 ounces (57g) cream cheese, at room temperature

1¼ cups (125g) powdered sugar

½ teaspoon almond extract

Pinch of salt

A drop or two of pink food coloring (optional)

1. Position a rack in the center of the oven and preheat to 350°F. Line an 8 × 8-inch baking pan with foil that hangs over two of the sides and lightly coat it with cooking spray or melted butter.

2. **MAKE THE BARS:** In a large bowl, whisk together the flour, granulated sugar, cardamom, baking powder, and salt until smooth. Add the melted butter, almond extract, and vanilla and stir with a spatula until just combined.

3. Transfer the dough to the prepared pan and press it into an even layer with your hands or a flat-bottomed measuring cup.

4. Bake until very light golden brown just at the edges, but still pale in the center, 20 to 22 minutes. Let the cookie bars cool in the pan on a rack. (While the bars are cooling, remove the butter and cream cheese for the frosting from the refrigerator and let them come to room temperature.)

5. **MEANWHILE, MAKE THE FROSTING:** In a large bowl, use a whisk (or an electric mixer if you have one) to beat the softened butter and cream cheese until smooth. Add the powdered sugar, almond extract, and salt and mix slowly until the sugar is incorporated. Once the sugar is incorporated, increase the speed and beat or whisk until smooth and fluffy. This will take a bit of muscle if you are mixing by hand, but it is doable. If desired, add food coloring and whisk it in.

6. Once cool, use the foil to lift the cookie bars out of the pan and remove the foil from the bars. Spread the frosting over the cooled bar and slice. Store in the fridge for about 4 days.

Cranberry Almond White Chocolate Bars

MAKES ONE 8 × 8-INCH PAN

These chewy bars are packed with almond flour, extract, and crispy sliced almonds on top for big almond flavor. The tart cranberries and creamy white chocolate are a nicely balanced pair, but bittersweet chocolate would be welcome at the party, too.

10 tablespoons (142g) unsalted butter, melted

1 cup (200g) packed light brown sugar

1 large egg, cold from the fridge

1 teaspoon almond extract

1 teaspoon vanilla extract

¾ teaspoon fine sea salt

½ teaspoon baking powder

¼ teaspoon baking soda

1 cup (128g) all-purpose flour

½ cup (50g) almond flour

¾ cup (100g) sweetened dried cranberries

½ cup (85g) white chocolate chips

½ cup (45g) sliced almonds

1. Position a rack in the center of the oven and preheat to 350°F. Coat an 8 × 8-inch baking pan with cooking spray or brush with butter. Line the pan with a strip of parchment paper that hangs over two of the sides.

2. In a large bowl, combine the melted butter and brown sugar and whisk until smooth. The mixture will start looking separated, but it will smooth out, about 30 seconds.

3. Add the egg, almond extract, vanilla, and salt and whisk until smooth and glossy.

4. Whisk in the baking powder and baking soda until combined and smooth. Fold in the all-purpose flour and the almond flour with a spatula. When a few streaks of flour remain, add the cranberries and all but about 2 tablespoons of the white chocolate chips and stir until just combined.

5. Transfer the dough to the prepared pan and smooth the top. Scatter the sliced almonds and the reserved white chocolate chips over the top.

6. Bake until golden brown all over and just a bit wiggly in the center, 27 to 32 minutes.

7. Let the bars cool in the pan on a rack, then use the parchment paper to lift the bars out of the pan and slice. Store in an airtight container at room temperature for up to 4 days.

Flavor Variations

BLUEBERRY ALMOND WHITE CHOCOLATE BARS: Substitute an equal amount of dried blueberries for the cranberries.

CHERRY ALMOND DARK CHOCOLATE BARS: Substitute an equal amount of dried cherries for the cranberries and dark chocolate chips for the white chocolate.

Ginger Cherry Oaties

Spicy ginger molasses cookies are one of my holiday must-haves and these bars incorporate all of those warm and delicious flavors. These bars add a bit of oatmeal and dried cherries for texture and a sweet-tart pop of flavor. I love them as is, but you can also add a handful of chocolate chips or make them super gingery by adding a bit of chopped crystallized ginger to the mix.

8 tablespoons (113g)
unsalted butter, melted

½ cup (100g) packed
light brown sugar

¼ cup (50g) granulated sugar

¼ cup (85g) unsulphured molasses

1 large egg, cold from the fridge

2 teaspoons ground ginger

1 teaspoon ground cinnamon

¼ teaspoon ground cloves

½ teaspoon fine sea salt

¾ teaspoon baking soda

1¾ cups (225g) all-purpose flour

½ cup (50g) old-fashioned rolled oats, plus more (optional) for topping

½ cup (75g) roughly chopped
dried cherries

1. Position a rack in the center of the oven and preheat to 350°F. Coat an 8 × 8-inch baking pan with cooking spray or brush with butter. Line the pan with a strip of parchment paper that hangs over two of the sides.

2. In a large bowl, combine the melted butter, brown sugar, granulated sugar, and molasses. Whisk until well combined and smooth, about 30 seconds.

3. Add the egg, ginger, cinnamon, cloves, and salt and whisk until smooth and glossy.

4. Whisk in the baking soda. Fold in the flour, oats, and cherries with a spatula. Mix until just combined and no streaks of flour remain.

5. Transfer the dough to the prepared pan and use an offset spatula or lightly oiled hands to press the sticky dough evenly into the pan. If desired, sprinkle a few more oats over the top.

6. Bake the bars until golden brown and just slightly firm, 24 to 27 minutes.

7. Let the bars cool in the pan on a rack, then use the parchment paper to lift the bars out of the pan and slice. Store in an airtight container at room temperature for up to 4 days.

Flavor Variations

CHOCOLATE GINGER OATIES: Omit the cherries and add ½ cup (85g), or up to 1 cup (170g), bittersweet chocolate chips or chopped bittersweet chocolate.

SUPER GINGER OATIES: Add ¼ cup (35g) finely chopped crystallized ginger when you add the flour and oats.

Loaded Chocolate Chip Cookie Bars

Is it a blondie or is it a cookie bar? Is there a difference? Does it matter? These bars are the sort that you can make even when it feels like there is nothing in the house. For the vegan butter, make sure to use sticks, rather than butter from a tub. If you're not vegan, you can also substitute dairy butter and conventional sugars and chocolate chips.

8 tablespoons (113g) unsalted vegan stick butter, melted, or ½ cup (95g) neutral oil

¾ cup (150g) organic light brown sugar

¼ cup (50g) organic cane sugar

¼ cup (60g) cold water

2 teaspoons vanilla extract

¾ teaspoon fine sea salt

¼ teaspoon baking powder

¼ teaspoon baking soda

1½ cups (190g) all-purpose flour

1 cup (170g) vegan chocolate chips, plus more (optional) for topping

½ cup (55g) chopped toasted walnuts, plus more (optional) for topping

½ cup (45g) unsweetened finely shredded toasted coconut (optional)

1. Position a rack in the center of the oven and preheat to 350°F. Coat an 8 × 8-inch baking pan with cooking spray or brush with oil. Line the pan with a strip of parchment paper that hangs over two of the sides.

2. In a large bowl, combine the melted butter, brown sugar, cane sugar, water, vanilla, and salt and whisk until smooth. The mixture will start out separated, but it will smooth out and come together.

3. Whisk in the baking powder and baking soda. Fold in the flour, chocolate chips, walnuts, and coconut (if using) with a spatula. Mix until no streaks of flour remain and the mix-ins are evenly distributed in the dough.

4. Transfer the dough to the prepared pan and use an offset spatula or lightly oiled hands to spread the sticky dough evenly into the pan. If desired, top with a sprinkle of additional chocolate and walnuts.

5. Bake the bars until golden brown and firm, with a tiny bit of give in the center, 30 to 40 minutes. They will puff up in the oven and sink a bit as they cool.

6. Let the bars cool in the pan on a rack, then use the parchment paper to lift the bars out of the pan and slice. Store in an airtight container at room temperature for up to 4 days.

Flavor Variations

CRANBERRY WHITE CHOCOLATE COOKIE BARS: Substitute an equal amount of white chocolate chips for the vegan chocolate chips. Substitute dried cranberries for the nuts.

BLUEBERRY PECAN COOKIE BARS: Omit the chocolate chips and add ½ cup (70g) dried blueberries. Substitute an equal amount of chopped toasted pecans for the walnuts.

Raspberry Mazurkas

Growing up, my mom owned a kids clothing and toy store in a cute neighborhood in Seattle. I'd often tag along with her to work, mostly because there was a coffee cart across the street run by two lovely sisters where we'd stop for a little something on the way in. She'd get a vanilla latte, I would get a steamed milk, and then we'd usually share a treat. Sometimes it was a peach/passion fruit scone, sometimes a Pink Cookie (page 101), and sometimes a nubbly little jam bar called a mazurka. I've never seen a mazurka outside of the coffee cart, but a little bit of research led me to learn that they are sometimes called Polish wedding cookies and were very popular in '90s Seattle.

1¼ cups (160g) all-purpose flour

1 cup (200g) packed light brown sugar

¾ cup (75g) old-fashioned rolled oats

⅔ cup (73g) finely chopped walnuts or pecans

½ cup (45g) unsweetened finely shredded coconut

¾ teaspoon fine sea salt

8 tablespoons (113g) unsalted butter, melted

1 cup (300g) raspberry preserves

1. Position a rack in the center of the oven and preheat to 325°F. Coat an 8 × 8-inch baking pan with cooking spray or brush with butter. Line the pan with two crossed strips of parchment paper that hang over the sides.

2. In a large bowl, combine the flour, brown sugar, oats, chopped nuts, coconut, and salt. Stir until well combined. Add the melted butter and stir until well combined and the mixture holds together in clumps. Use your fingers to do the last bit of mixing.

3. Measure out about 1 heaping cup of the mixture and set aside. Transfer the rest to the prepared pan and gently and evenly press the mixture into the bottom of the pan.

4. Spread the jam evenly over the top. Sprinkle the reserved crumbs over the jam and very gently press them in.

5. Bake until the top is deep golden brown and the jam just starts to bubble around the edges, 40 to 50 minutes.

6. Let the bars cool completely in the pan on a rack, then use the parchment paper to lift the bars out of the pan and slice. Store in an airtight container at room temperature for up to 4 days.

Flavor Variation

APRICOT MAZURKAS: Substitute your favorite fruit preserves for the raspberry—something a little tart like apricot is delicious. Add a bit of citrus zest to the crumble, if you'd like.

Banana Nut Blondies

These have all of the flavors of your favorite banana bread in a more compact form. They are just sweet enough, with lots of toasty walnuts inside and on top. Chocolate and banana are such good pals, they would be great with some chocolate chips, too. Feel free to use dairy butter if you don't avoid dairy.

8 tablespoons (113g) unsalted vegan stick butter, melted, or ½ cup (125g) liquid coconut oil

¾ cup (150g) organic light brown sugar

½ cup (125g) mashed very ripe banana (about 1 banana)

1 teaspoon vanilla extract

½ teaspoon fine sea salt

¼ teaspoon baking powder

¼ teaspoon baking soda

1½ cups (190g) all-purpose flour

¾ cup (83g) chopped toasted walnuts

1. Position a rack in the center of the oven and preheat to 350°F. Coat an 8 × 8-inch baking pan with cooking spray. Line the pan with a strip of parchment paper that hangs over two of the edges.

2. In a large bowl, whisk the melted butter, brown sugar, banana, vanilla, and salt until combined, about 30 seconds.

3. Whisk in the baking powder and baking soda. Fold in the flour and ½ cup (55g) of the walnuts with a spatula and mix until well combined. The batter will be very thick.

4. Spoon the batter into the prepared pan and spread in an even layer. Sprinkle the remaining ¼ cup (28g) walnuts on top.

5. Bake the blondies until slightly puffed and golden and a tester inserted into the center comes out clean, 25 to 30 minutes.

6. Let the blondies cool in the pan on a rack for about 15 minutes, then use the parchment paper to lift the cake out and onto the rack to cool completely before slicing. Store loosely covered at room temperature or in the fridge for up to 3 days.

Flavor Variation

CHOCOLATE BANANA NUT BLONDIES: Add up to 1 cup (170g) vegan chocolate chips when you add the nuts.

Coffee-Glazed Molasses Bars

I love a molasses cookie any time of year, and these chewy bar cookies are packed with all of the delicious warm spices you'd expect. The coffee glaze is pleasantly bittersweet, just like molasses, and they make such a tasty pair you'll be left wondering why all molasses cookies don't have a little coffee glaze on top.

Molasses Bars

8 tablespoons (113g) unsalted butter, melted

⅓ cup (113g) unsulphured molasses

½ cup (100g) packed light brown sugar

¼ cup (50g) granulated sugar

1 large egg, cold from the fridge

2 teaspoons ground cinnamon

2 teaspoons ground ginger

½ teaspoon ground allspice

½ teaspoon fine sea salt

¾ teaspoon baking soda

1½ cups (190g) all-purpose flour

Coffee Glaze

½ cup (50g) powdered sugar

1 teaspoon instant espresso powder

Pinch of salt

2 to 3 teaspoons milk, any kind

1. Position a rack in the center of the oven and preheat to 350°F. Coat an 8 × 8-inch baking pan with cooking spray or brush with butter. Line the pan with a strip of parchment paper that hangs over two of the sides.

2. **MAKE THE BARS:** In a large bowl, combine the melted butter, molasses, brown sugar, and granulated sugar. Whisk until well combined, about 30 seconds.

3. Add the egg, cinnamon, ginger, allspice, and salt and whisk until smooth and glossy.

4. Whisk in the baking soda. Fold in the flour with a spatula and mix until combined and no streaks of flour remain.

5. Transfer the dough to the prepared pan and use an offset spatula or lightly oiled hands to press the thick dough evenly into the pan.

6. Bake the bars until puffy, golden brown, and just slightly firm, 24 to 27 minutes.

7. Let the bars cool in the pan on a rack; they will deflate as they cool.

8. **MEANWHILE, MAKE THE GLAZE:** In a medium bowl, whisk together the powdered sugar, espresso powder, and salt. Drizzle in the milk until the glaze is thick and opaque but pourable.

9. Use the parchment paper to lift the bars out of the pan and then drizzle the glaze evenly over the cooled bars. Let the glaze set for a few minutes before slicing. Store in an airtight container at room temperature for up to 4 days.

Flavor Variations

GINGER MOLASSES WHITE CHOCOLATE BARS: Fold in ¾ cup (128g) white chocolate chips or chopped white chocolate and ½ cup (70g) chopped crystallized ginger when you add the flour. Omit the glaze.

BUTTER RUM MOLASSES BARS: Omit the coffee glaze and drizzle the bars with the butter rum glaze from Glazed Cookie Butter Bars (page 98).

Pumpkin Chocolate Chip Bars

MAKES ONE 8 × 8-INCH PAN

A little cakey, a little spicy, a little pumpkin-y and chocolatey, these bars have lots to love. This is my favorite combination of warm spices, with a little bit of cardamom and allspice added to their more familiar friends, cinnamon and ginger.

8 tablespoons (113g) unsalted butter, melted

1 cup (200g) packed light brown sugar

⅓ cup (75g) canned unsweetened pumpkin puree

1 tablespoon neutral oil

1 teaspoon vanilla extract

2 teaspoons ground cinnamon

1 teaspoon ground ginger

½ teaspoon ground cardamom

¼ teaspoon ground allspice

½ teaspoon fine sea salt

½ teaspoon baking soda

1½ cups (190g) all-purpose flour

1 cup (170g) semisweet chocolate chips

1. Position a rack in the center of the oven and preheat to 350°F. Coat an 8 × 8-inch baking pan with cooking spray or brush with butter. Line the pan with a strip of parchment paper that hangs over two of the sides.

2. In a large bowl, combine the melted butter and brown sugar and whisk until well combined, about 30 seconds.

3. Add the pumpkin, oil, vanilla, cinnamon, ginger, cardamom, allspice, and salt and whisk until smooth and glossy.

4. Whisk in the baking soda. Fold in the flour and ¾ cup (128g) of the chocolate chips with a spatula. Mix until just combined.

5. Transfer the dough to the prepared pan and use an offset spatula to spread the sticky dough evenly into the pan. Use a bit of oil or cooking spray if necessary to keep the dough from sticking. Sprinkle the remaining ¼ cup (42g) chocolate chips over the top and press them gently into the surface.

6. Bake the bars until light golden brown and just slightly firm, with a tiny bit of wiggle in the center, 30 to 35 minutes. They will puff up in the oven, then sink a bit as they cool.

7. Let the bars cool in the pan on a rack for about 20 minutes, then use the parchment paper to lift the bars out of the pan and slice. Store in an airtight container at room temperature for up to 4 days.

Flavor Variation

PUMPKIN SPICE LATTE BARS: Top the cooled bars with a drizzle of the coffee glaze from Coffee-Glazed Molasses Bars (page 112).

Chocolate Cherry Pistachio Bars

Bright green pistachios and deep red cherries give these super-chocolatey bars gorgeous color and chewy crunchy textures. These definitely lean more toward a toothsome cookie bar than fudgy brownie, and any chocolate lover in your life would be happy for a slice alongside their afternoon coffee.

8 tablespoons (113g) unsalted butter, melted

½ cup (100g) granulated sugar

½ cup (100g) packed light brown sugar

2 tablespoons neutral oil

1 teaspoon vanilla extract

½ teaspoon fine sea salt

1 large egg, cold from the fridge

⅔ cup (60g) Dutch process cocoa powder, sifted if lumpy

½ teaspoon baking powder

¾ cup (96g) all-purpose flour

½ cup (75g) roughly chopped dried cherries

¾ cup (128g) chopped chocolate or chocolate chips, any kind you like

8 tablespoons (60g) chopped toasted pistachios

1. Position a rack in the center of the oven and preheat to 350°F. Coat an 8 × 8-inch baking pan with cooking spray or brush with butter. Line the pan with a strip of parchment paper that hangs over two of the sides.

2. In a large bowl, combine the melted butter, granulated sugar, brown sugar, oil, vanilla, and salt and whisk until combined, about 30 seconds.

3. Add the egg and whisk until smooth and glossy.

4. Whisk in the cocoa powder until smooth. Whisk in the baking powder. Fold in the flour, cherries, ½ cup (85g) of the chocolate chips, and 6 tablespoons (45g) of the chopped pistachios with a spatula. Mix just until no streaks of flour remain. Don't overmix.

5. Transfer the batter to the prepared pan and spread in an even layer. Sprinkle the remaining ¼ cup (43g) chocolate and 2 tablespoons (15g) pistachios over the top.

6. Bake the bars until set and matte with a few cracks around the edges, 28 to 33 minutes.

7. Let the bars cool completely in the pan on a rack, then run a thin knife or offset spatula along the edges of the pan that are not protected by the parchment, and use the parchment paper to lift the bars out of the pan and slice. Store in an airtight container at room temperature for up to 4 days.

Flavor Variations

CHOCOLATE CHERRY WALNUT BARS: Substitute an equal amount of chopped toasted walnuts (or any other nut) for the pistachios.

SUPER CHOCOLATE CHERRY BARS: Omit the pistachios and add an additional ¼ cup (43g) chocolate to the batter.

Peanut Butter Blondies

I love to add a hefty dose of peanut butter chips to these crisp and chewy bars for extra creamy peanut buttery goodness, but you can just as easily sub in chocolate chips. Use a conventional peanut butter like Skippy or Jif for the best results. These also make an excellent brookie (see Make It a Brookie, page 124).

8 tablespoons (113g) unsalted butter, melted

1 cup (200g) packed light brown sugar

½ cup (125g) creamy or chunky conventional peanut butter

1 large egg, cold from the fridge

1 teaspoon vanilla extract

½ teaspoon fine sea salt

¼ teaspoon baking powder

¼ teaspoon baking soda

1 cup (128g) all-purpose flour

1 cup (170g) peanut butter chips or chocolate chips

½ cup (55g) chopped salted peanuts

1. Position a rack in the center of the oven and preheat to 350°F. Coat an 8 × 8-inch baking pan with cooking spray or brush with butter. Line the pan with a strip of parchment paper that hangs over two of the sides.

2. In a large bowl, combine the melted butter, brown sugar, and peanut butter and whisk until smooth, about 30 seconds.

3. Add the egg, vanilla, and salt, and whisk until smooth and glossy.

4. Whisk in the baking powder and baking soda. Fold in the flour, peanut butter chips, and ¼ cup (27g) of the peanuts with a spatula.

5. Transfer the batter to the prepared pan and spread in an even layer. Sprinkle the remaining ¼ cup (27g) peanuts over the top.

6. Bake until golden brown all over and just a bit wiggly in the center, 25 to 30 minutes.

7. Let the blondies cool in the pan on a rack, then use the parchment paper to lift the bars out of the pan and slice. Store in an airtight container at room temperature for up to 4 days.

Flavor Variations

PEANUT BUTTER CUP BLONDIES: Substitute chopped peanut butter cups for the peanut butter chips.

CHOCOLATE PEANUT BUTTER BLONDIES: Use half peanut butter chips and half chocolate chips (any kind you like).

Coconut Cookie Bark

Part chewy macaroon, part crispy shortbread, this big ol' cookie has it all. Bake it until it is golden brown, then use your hands to break it into whatever size cookie you need at the moment. The coconut extract is optional but adds lots of delicious flavor; if you choose not to use it, add an additional ½ teaspoon vanilla.

8 tablespoons (113g) unsalted butter, melted

⅔ cup plus 2 tablespoons (192g) granulated sugar

1 teaspoon coconut extract (optional)

1 teaspoon vanilla extract

½ teaspoon fine sea salt

½ teaspoon baking soda

1 cup (128g) all-purpose flour

½ cup (45g) unsweetened finely shredded coconut

1. Position a rack in the center of the oven and preheat to 350°F. Line a large, rimmed baking sheet with parchment paper.

2. In a large bowl, combine the melted butter and ⅔ cup (167g) of the sugar and whisk until well combined, about 30 seconds.

3. Add the coconut extract (if using), vanilla, and salt and whisk until smooth.

4. Whisk in the baking soda. Fold in the flour and shredded coconut with a spatula and mix until just combined. The dough will be thick and a bit crumbly.

5. Transfer the mixture to the prepared pan and press the dough into a thin even round just under ¼ inch thick. You should have a roughly 10-inch round cookie, but it doesn't need to be perfect. If the mixture is crumbly around the edges, use your fingertips to press the edges together. Sprinkle the remaining 2 tablespoons (25g) sugar over the top and press gently.

6. Bake until golden brown and firm to the touch, 18 to 20 minutes.

7. Let cool completely on the pan, then use your hands to break the cookie into pieces. Store in an airtight container at room temperature for up to 4 days.

Flavor Variation

COFFEE COCONUT COOKIE BARK: Add 2 teaspoons instant espresso powder and an additional ½ teaspoon vanilla extract.

Triple-Chocolate Olive Oil Brownies

These brownies may be dairy-free, but they aren't missing a single thing. They are super rich and fudgy and come together quickly with a heavy dose of Dutch process cocoa and a healthy bit of chocolate folded into the batter. Cut them into tiny squares and enjoy with a warm cozy beverage. They are also great straight from the freezer in the middle of the night . . . not that I would know or anything. You can mix in any type of chocolate that you like. If you are not avoiding dairy, try a mix of bittersweet and milk, but white chocolate would be great, too.

¾ cup (143g) mild-tasting olive oil

1½ cups (300g) granulated sugar

¾ cup (68g) Dutch process cocoa powder, sifted if lumpy

¾ teaspoon fine sea salt

2 teaspoons vanilla extract

3 large eggs, cold from the fridge

¾ cup (96g) all-purpose flour

½ cup (85g) chopped bittersweet chocolate

½ cup (85g) chopped semisweet or milk chocolate

Flaky sea salt (optional), for sprinkling

1. Position a rack in the center of the oven and preheat to 350°F. Coat an 8 × 8-inch baking pan with cooking spray or brush with oil. Line the pan with a strip of parchment paper that hangs over two of the sides. Spray or oil the parchment paper.

2. In a large bowl, whisk together the olive oil, sugar, cocoa, fine sea salt, and vanilla. The mixture will seize a bit, but keep whisking until the mixture is well combined and no lumps in the cocoa remain, about 30 seconds.

3. Add the eggs and whisk vigorously until smooth and glossy, about 30 seconds.

4. Fold in the flour with a spatula and mix until a few streaks of flour remain. Add the chopped chocolates, reserving a few tablespoons to sprinkle on the top.

5. Pour the batter into the prepared pan and smooth the top. Sprinkle the reserved chocolate and flaky salt (if using) over the top.

6. Bake the brownies until set and slightly firm with a few cracks on top, 33 to 38 minutes.

7. Let the brownies cool in the pan on a rack, then use the parchment paper to lift the brownies out of the pan and cut into small squares. Store in an airtight container in the fridge at room temperature for up to 4 days.

Flavor Variations

PEANUT BUTTERY OLIVE OIL BROWNIES: Fold in a handful of peanut butter chips or chopped up peanut butter cups when you add the chopped chocolates.

NUTTY OLIVE OIL BROWNIES: Fold in ⅔ cup (73g) chopped toasted walnuts or pecans when you add the chopped chocolates.

MALTED OLIVE OIL BROWNIES: Fold in ¼ cup (30g) malted milk powder when you add the flour.

make it a brookie!

What's a brookie you ask? Well, it's when you combine two of the world's best baked goods—cookies and brownies—into one glorious treat. Usually they are made with chocolate chip cookie dough, but you can really make them with any drop cookie dough you like. To make a batch of brookies, butter or coat a 9 × 13-inch pan with cooking spray and line it with a sheet of parchment paper that hangs over the two long sides. Make one batch of batter for Chewy Cocoa Brownies (page 86) and one batch of cookie or bar dough—try New Favorite Chocolate Chip Cookies (page 61) or Peanut Butter Blondies (page 119). Spoon alternating dollops of brownie batter and cookie dough into the pan. Press the cookie dough down lightly and use a knife to swirl the brownie batter into the cookie dough a little bit. It's okay if there are a few small gaps here and there; they will sort themselves out in the oven. If you like, sprinkle some chopped chocolate or nuts over the top. Bake in a 350°F oven until the brownie batter is just set and the cookie dough is golden and cooked through, 25 to 30 minutes. Let the bars cool in the pan on a rack as long as you can stand it before diving in.

Date and Pistachio Coffee Bars

Caramelly dates are one of my very favorite foods and they pair so well with bitter coffee, toasty pistachios, and nutty sweet coconut in these bars. Somehow the combination smells just like pancakes and maple syrup (I don't know why, it just does!). Dates are quite sticky, so I like to snip them with kitchen shears rather than cut them with a knife. Feel free to swap the nuts for whatever type you like, and add a handful of chocolate chips while you're at it.

8 tablespoons (113g) unsalted butter, melted

1 cup (200g) packed dark brown sugar

1 teaspoon instant espresso powder

1 large egg, cold from the fridge

1 teaspoon vanilla extract

½ teaspoon fine sea salt

¼ teaspoon baking powder

¼ teaspoon baking soda

1 cup (128g) all-purpose flour

½ cup (70g) chopped pitted dates

½ cup (60g) chopped toasted pistachios

½ cup (45g) unsweetened finely shredded coconut

1. Position a rack in the center of the oven and preheat to 350°F. Coat an 8 × 8-inch baking pan with cooking spray or brush with butter. Line the pan with a strip of parchment paper that hangs over two of the sides.

2. In a large bowl, combine the melted butter, brown sugar, and espresso powder and whisk for 30 seconds.

3. Add the egg, vanilla, and salt and stir until smooth and glossy.

4. Whisk in the baking powder and baking soda. Fold in the flour, dates, 6 tablespoons (45g) of the pistachios and 6 tablespoons (34g) of the coconut with a spatula. Mix until no streaks of flour remain.

5. Transfer the batter to the prepared pan and spread in an even layer. Sprinkle the remaining 2 tablespoons each of pistachios and coconut over the top.

6. Bake the bars until golden brown, set, and matte with a few cracks around the edges, 28 to 33 minutes.

7. Let the bars cool in the pan on a rack, then run a thin knife or offset spatula along the edges of the pan that are not protected by the parchment, and use the parchment paper to lift the brownies out of the pan and slice. Store in an airtight container at room temperature for up to 4 days, or a few days longer in the fridge.

Flavor Variation

CHOCOLATEY DATE AND PISTACHIO COFFEE BARS: Add ½ cup (85g) chopped chocolate or chocolate chips when you add the dates, pistachios, and coconut.

cakes

How could I write a collection of "snacking bakes" without including my favorite little snacking cakes? This chapter is full of the easy cakes that you know and love. They are all one-layer cakes that can be baked in an 8 × 8-inch square or a 9-inch round pan, perfect for an afternoon snack or anytime treat. Some of them have a quick and easy topping like a glaze or frosting, and some have no topping at all, but feel free to mix and match the cakes and toppings to your heart's content.

Chocolate Chip Snickerdoodle Cake

Cinnamon and sugar is a classic and delicious flavor combination that lends itself perfectly to cake. Here, sour cream adds the signature snickerdoodle tang, and I've added chocolate chips because, well, what isn't better with a little bit of chocolate? Feel free to add a few more tablespoons of chips on top of the batter before you sprinkle the cinnamon sugar for bigger chocolate flavor.

¾ cup (150g) plus 2 tablespoons granulated sugar

1 teaspoon ground cinnamon

2 large eggs

¾ cup (173g) sour cream

½ cup (95g) neutral oil

½ teaspoon fine sea salt

1½ teaspoons baking powder

½ teaspoon baking soda

1¾ cups (225g) all-purpose flour

½ cup (85g) semisweet chocolate chips

1. Position a rack in the center of the oven and preheat to 350°F. Coat an 8 × 8-inch baking pan with cooking spray or brush with butter. Line the pan with a strip of parchment paper that hangs over two of the edges. Very lightly butter or spray the parchment.

2. In a small bowl, combine 2 tablespoons of the sugar and the cinnamon. Sprinkle the bottom and sides of the pan with half of the cinnamon-sugar mixture.

3. In a large bowl, whisk together the remaining ¾ cup (150g) sugar and eggs until pale and foamy, about 1 minute. Add the sour cream, oil, and salt and whisk until smooth and emulsified.

4. Whisk in the baking powder and baking soda. Fold in the flour and chocolate chips with a spatula and mix until well combined.

5. Pour the batter into the prepared pan, smooth the top, and sprinkle the remaining cinnamon sugar over the top.

6. Bake the cake until puffed and golden and a tester inserted into the center comes out clean or with a bit of melted chocolate, 30 to 40 minutes.

7. Let the cake cool in the pan on a rack for about 15 minutes, then use the parchment paper to lift the cake out of the pan and onto the rack to cool. Store loosely covered at room temperature for up to 3 days.

Flavor Variations

EXTRA CINNAMONY SNICKERDOODLE CAKE: Reduce the cinnamon sugar mixture by half and use it only to coat the bottom and sides of the pan. While the cake is baking, make a cinnamon glaze by stirring together 1 cup (100g) powdered sugar, 2 teaspoons ground cinnamon, 3 to 4 teaspoons milk, and a pinch of salt. Drizzle the glaze over the cooled cake.

RASPBERRY CHOCOLATE CHIP SNICKERDOODLE CAKE: Add 1 cup (130g) fresh raspberries when you add the chocolate chips. Fold gently to combine.

Use Another Pan

MUFFINS/CUPCAKES: Line a muffin tin with paper liners and fill the cups two-thirds full. Sprinkle the top of each cupcake with the cinnamon sugar. Bake until puffed and a tester inserted into the center comes out clean, about 20 minutes. Makes 12 to 18 muffins/cupcakes.

SHEET: Make a double batch of the batter and cinnamon sugar and bake in a 9 × 13-inch baking pan until puffed and a tester inserted into the center comes out clean, 40 to 50 minutes.

Peanut Butter and Jam Cake with Raspberries

Peanut butter and jam are great friends in a sandwich and are even better in this cake. Here, sweet and tart raspberry jam is swirled through a perfectly tender peanut butter and sour cream cake. I love using raspberry jam and some fresh raspberries here, but blackberries would be delicious, too, or even grapes when Concord grapes are in season (just seed the grapes first). Use creamy conventional peanut butter like Skippy or Jif for the best texture.

¾ cup (150g) granulated sugar

2 large eggs

¾ cup (173g) sour cream

½ cup (125g) creamy conventional peanut butter

8 tablespoons (113g) unsalted butter, melted

2 teaspoons vanilla extract

½ teaspoon fine sea salt

1½ teaspoons baking powder

½ teaspoon baking soda

1¼ cups (160g) all-purpose flour

⅓ cup (90g) raspberry jam

½ cup (70g) fresh raspberries (optional)

1. Position a rack in the center of the oven and preheat to 350°F. Coat an 8 × 8-inch baking pan with cooking spray or brush with butter. Line the pan with a strip of parchment paper that hangs over two of the edges.

2. In a large bowl, whisk the sugar and eggs until pale and foamy, about 1 minute. Add the sour cream, peanut butter, melted butter, vanilla, and salt and whisk until smooth and emulsified.

3. Whisk in the baking powder and baking soda. Fold in the flour with a spatula and mix until well combined.

4. Pour the batter into the prepared pan, smooth the top, then dot the top with the jam. Use a skewer or thin knife to swirl the jam through the batter. If desired, scatter the raspberries over the top.

5. Bake the cake until puffed and golden and a tester inserted into the center comes out clean, 40 to 50 minutes. This cake can be tricky to test for doneness, so try to choose a spot without jam to test.

6. Let the cake cool in the pan on a rack for about 15 minutes, then use the parchment paper to lift the cake out and onto the rack to cool completely. Store loosely covered at room temperature for up to 3 days.

Flavor Variation

PEANUT BUTTER AND JAM CAKE WITH BLACKBERRIES: Substitute blackberry jam and fresh blackberries for the raspberry jam and raspberries.

Use Another Pan

SHEET: Make a double batch of the batter and double the fresh raspberries (if using). Bake in a 9 × 13-inch pan until puffed and a tester inserted into the center comes out clean, 50 to 60 minutes.

Brown Butter Marble Cake

This diner classic gets a little boost from one of my favorite ingredients, brown butter. Browning the butter takes about 5 minutes, but it adds so much flavor to this marbled chocolate and vanilla cake. It is great as is or topped with a little powdered sugar, but it's also delicious with a bit of berry jam swirled in or mocha glaze on top.

10 tablespoons (142g) cold unsalted butter, cut into tablespoons

¾ cup (150g) granulated sugar

2 large eggs

1 cup (230g) sour cream

1 teaspoon vanilla extract

½ teaspoon fine sea salt

1½ teaspoons baking powder

½ teaspoon baking soda

1¼ cups (160g) all-purpose flour

3 tablespoons Dutch process cocoa powder, sifted if lumpy

Powdered sugar, for dusting

1. Position a rack in the center of the oven and preheat to 350°F. Coat an 8 × 8-inch baking pan with cooking spray or brush with butter. Line the pan with a strip of parchment paper that hangs over two of the edges.

2. In a small skillet or saucepan with a light-colored interior, melt 8 tablespoons (113g) of the butter over medium heat. Once melted, cook the butter, stirring constantly until the milk solids are deep golden brown, about 3 minutes. Remove from the heat and add the remaining 2 tablespoons (29g) cold butter to the pan and swirl until the butter melts.

3. In a large bowl, whisk the granulated sugar and eggs until pale and foamy, about 1 minute. Add the sour cream, brown butter, vanilla, and salt and whisk until smooth and emulsified.

4. Whisk in the baking powder and baking soda. Fold in the flour with a spatula and mix until well combined. Scoop about 1¼ cups of batter into a medium bowl and stir in the cocoa powder until smooth.

5. Scoop alternating dollops of each batter into the prepared pan and use a skewer to swirl the two batters together. Tap the pan on the counter a few times to settle the batter in the pan.

6. Bake the cake until puffed and golden and a tester inserted into the center comes out clean or with a few chocolatey crumbs, 30 to 35 minutes.

7. Let the cake cool in the pan on a rack for about 15 minutes, then use the parchment paper to lift the cake out and onto the rack to cool completely. If desired, dust with powdered sugar before serving. Store loosely covered at room temperature for up to 3 days.

Flavor Variations

JAMMY MARBLE CAKE: Dollop ½ cup (135g) raspberry jam over the top of the cake after you scoop the two batters in the pan, but before you swirl. Swirl the batters and jam together, then bake the cake as directed.

MOCHA MARBLE CAKE: Add 1 teaspoon instant espresso powder to the batter along with the vanilla. Top the cooled cake with the mocha glaze from Mocha Banana Cake (page 151).

Use Another Pan

LOAF: Bake in a 9 × 5 × 3-inch loaf pan until puffed and golden brown and a tester inserted into the center comes out clean, 45 to 55 minutes.

SHEET: Make a double batch of the batter and bake in a 9 × 13-inch pan until puffed and a tester inserted into the center comes out clean, 40 to 50 minutes.

Cornmeal Carrot Cake

Carrot cake is one of my very favorites and this egg- and dairy-free version is lightly spiced with a little bit of extra texture thanks to some cornmeal in the batter. Feel free to add about ½ cup (55g) chopped toasted nuts and some raisins, too, if that's your thing. If you're not worried about keeping it vegan, frost the cooled cake with the cream cheese frosting from the Pink Cookie Bars (page 101) with a little squeeze of lemon juice added to the frosting.

¾ cup (150g) organic cane sugar

½ cup (95g) neutral oil

½ cup (120g) unsweetened nondairy milk, any kind

1 tablespoon apple cider vinegar

1 teaspoon ground cinnamon

½ teaspoon ground ginger

½ teaspoon freshly grated nutmeg

½ teaspoon fine sea salt

1½ teaspoons baking powder

½ teaspoon baking soda

1½ cups (190g) all-purpose flour

½ cup (70g) fine cornmeal

2 cups (225g) grated peeled carrots (about 4 medium), grated on the large holes of a box grater

1. Position a rack in the center of the oven and preheat to 350°F. Coat an 8 × 8-inch baking pan with cooking spray or brush with butter. Line the pan with a strip of parchment paper that hangs over two of the edges.

2. In a large bowl, whisk the sugar, oil, milk, vinegar, cinnamon, ginger, nutmeg, and salt until well combined.

3. Whisk in the baking powder and baking soda. Fold in the flour and cornmeal with a spatula and mix until a few streaks of flour remain. Fold in the carrots and mix until well combined. The batter will be thick.

4. Spoon the batter into the prepared pan and spread in an even layer. Tap the pan on the counter a few times to settle the batter in the pan.

5. Bake the cake until puffed and golden and a tester inserted into the center comes out clean, 35 to 40 minutes.

6. Let the cake cool in the pan on a rack for about 15 minutes, then use the parchment paper to lift the cake out and onto the rack to cool completely. Store loosely covered at room temperature for up to 3 days.

Flavor Variations

ZUCCHINI CORNMEAL CAKE: Substitute an equal amount of shredded and gently squeezed zucchini for the carrot.

LEMONY GLAZED CORNMEAL CARROT CAKE: Top the cooled cake with the lemon almond glaze from Lemon Almond Poppy Seed Cake (page 158), but omit the almond extract.

Use Another Pan

MUFFINS/CUPCAKES: Line a muffin tin with paper liners and fill the cups two-thirds full. Bake until puffed and a tester inserted into the center comes out clean, about 20 minutes. Makes 12 to 18 muffins/cupcakes.

ROUND: Bake in a 9-inch round pan until puffed and a tester inserted into the center comes out clean, 35 to 40 minutes.

Spiced Applesauce Crumb Cake

This cozy, streusel-topped applesauce cake is moist and lightly spiced, perfect for a little afternoon snack and then breakfast the next day. The streusel topping is buttery and delicious, but make sure to use vegan butter sticks, rather than the butter from a tub for the best texture.

Streusel

½ cup (64g) all-purpose flour

¼ cup (50g) organic light brown sugar

3 tablespoons (42g) cold unsalted vegan stick butter, cut into tablespoons

Pinch of salt

Spiced Apple Cake

⅔ cup (133g) organic cane sugar

½ cup (95g) neutral oil

½ cup (135g) unsweetened applesauce

1½ teaspoons ground cinnamon

1 teaspoon ground ginger

½ teaspoon freshly grated nutmeg

½ teaspoon fine sea salt

¼ teaspoon finely grated orange zest

1 teaspoon baking powder

½ teaspoon baking soda

1½ cups (190g) all-purpose flour

Organic powdered sugar (optional), for dusting

1. Position a rack in the center of the oven and preheat to 350°F. Coat an 8 × 8-inch baking pan with cooking spray or brush with oil. Line the pan with a strip of parchment paper that hangs over two of the edges.

2. **MAKE THE STREUSEL:** In a small bowl, combine the flour, brown sugar, butter, and salt. Pinch the mixture together with your fingertips until the mixture is well combined and crumbs form.

3. **MAKE THE CAKE:** In a large bowl, whisk the sugar, oil, applesauce, cinnamon, ginger, nutmeg, salt, and orange zest until smooth.

4. Whisk in the baking powder and baking soda. Fold in the flour with a spatula and mix until well combined.

5. Spoon the batter into the prepared pan and smooth the top. Tap the pan on the counter a few times to help the batter settle and remove any air bubbles. Sprinkle the streusel evenly over the top.

6. Bake the cake until puffed and golden and a tester inserted into the center comes out clean, 30 to 40 minutes.

7. Let the cake cool in the pan on a rack for about 15 minutes, then use the parchment paper to lift the cake out and onto the rack to cool completely. If desired, dust with powdered sugar before serving. Store loosely covered at room temperature for up to 3 days.

Flavor Variations

PEAR STREUSEL COFFEE CAKE: Substitute an equal amount of pear sauce for the applesauce. Add ½ teaspoon ground cardamom when you add the other spices.

PUMPKIN STREUSEL COFFEE CAKE: Substitute an equal amount of unsweetened pumpkin puree for the applesauce.

Use Another Pan

ROUND: Bake in a 9-inch round pan until puffed and a tester inserted into the center comes out clean, 30 to 40 minutes.

SHEET: Make a double batch of the batter and streusel and bake in a 9 × 13-inch pan until puffed and a tester inserted into the center comes out clean, 40 to 50 minutes.

Chocolate Ricotta Cake

This cake leans toward brownie territory in the best possible way. It is rich and dense, but not too sweet. The bit of cardamom gives it a depth of flavor that you might not be able to put your finger on, but you'd miss if it wasn't there. This cake is excellent on its own with a gentle shower of powdered sugar over the top or you can mix and match with a glaze or frosting from another recipe.

1¼ cups (250g) granulated sugar

2 large eggs

¾ cup (173g) whole-milk ricotta

½ cup (95g) neutral oil or mild-tasting olive oil

2 teaspoons vanilla extract

1 teaspoon ground cardamom

½ teaspoon fine sea salt

¾ cup (67g) Dutch process cocoa powder, sifted if lumpy

1½ teaspoons baking powder

½ teaspoon baking soda

1 cup (128g) all-purpose flour

Powdered sugar (optional), for dusting

1. Position a rack in the center of the oven and preheat to 350°F. Coat an 8 × 8-inch baking pan with cooking spray or brush with butter. Line the pan with a strip of parchment paper that hangs over two of the edges.

2. In a large bowl, whisk the granulated sugar and eggs until pale and foamy, about 1 minute. Add the ricotta, oil, vanilla, cardamom, and salt and whisk until smooth and emulsified.

3. Whisk in the cocoa powder until smooth. Whisk in the baking powder and baking soda. Fold in the flour with a spatula and mix until well combined.

4. Pour the batter into the prepared pan and smooth the top. Bake the cake until puffed and a tester inserted into the center comes out clean, 45 to 55 minutes.

5. Let the cake cool in the pan on a rack for about 15 minutes, then use the parchment paper to lift the cake out and onto the rack to cool completely. If desired, dust with powdered sugar before slicing. Store loosely covered at room temperature for up to 3 days.

Flavor Variations

MOCHA RICOTTA CAKE: Top the cooled cake with the mocha glaze from Mocha Banana Cake (page 151).

RASPBERRY CHOCOLATE RICOTTA CAKE: Sprinkle 1 cup (140g) fresh raspberries on top of the batter before baking.

CHOCOLATE CREAM CHEESE FROSTED RICOTTA CAKE: Frost the cooled cake with a double batch of the cream cheese frosting from Pink Cookie Bars (page 101). Or make it a chocolate cream cheese frosting by adding ¼ cup (23g) Dutch process cocoa powder to it and top with rainbow sprinkles.

Use Another Pan

MUFFINS/CUPCAKES: Line a muffin tin with paper liners and fill the cups two-thirds full. Bake until puffed and a tester inserted into the center comes out clean, about 20 minutes. Makes 12 to 18 muffins/cupcakes.

Walnut Cream Cheese Coffee Cake

This extra-cozy coffee cake has a secret. Along with the crisp and crunchy crumble topping, there is a layer of brown sugary goodness and rich cream cheese running through the center. Enjoy this cake warm just as it comes out of the oven, or bake it in the evening and reward yourself with a very tasty breakfast.

Walnut Cinnamon Crumble

½ cup (100g) packed light brown sugar

½ cup (64g) all-purpose flour

½ cup (60g) chopped toasted walnuts

¼ cup (25g) old-fashioned rolled oats

2 teaspoons ground cinnamon

Pinch of salt

4 tablespoons (56g) unsalted butter, melted

Sour Cream Coffee Cake

¾ cup (150g) granulated sugar

2 large eggs

¾ cup (173g) sour cream

8 tablespoons (113g) unsalted butter, melted

½ teaspoon fine sea salt

1½ teaspoons baking powder

½ teaspoon baking soda

1½ cups (190g) all-purpose flour

2 ounces (57g) cold cream cheese

1. Position a rack in the center of the oven and preheat to 350°F. Coat an 8 × 8-inch baking pan with cooking spray or brush with butter. Line the pan with a strip of parchment paper that hangs over two of the edges.

2. **MAKE THE CRUMBLE:** In a medium bowl, combine the brown sugar, flour, walnuts, oats, cinnamon, and salt and stir to combine. Add the melted butter and stir until combined. The mixture will be sandy.

3. **MAKE THE CAKE:** In a large bowl, whisk the granulated sugar and eggs until pale and foamy, about 1 minute. Add the sour cream, butter, and salt and whisk until smooth and emulsified.

4. Whisk in the baking powder and baking soda. Fold in the all-purpose flour with a spatula and mix to combine.

5. Spoon half of the batter into the prepared pan and smooth the top. Use your fingers to break the cream cheese into teaspoon-size pieces and scatter them over the top of the batter. Sprinkle half of the walnut crumble on top. Spoon the rest of the batter over the crumble and use an offset spatula or spoon to gently smooth the batter. Sprinkle the remaining walnut crumble on top.

6. Bake the cake until puffed and golden and a tester inserted into the center comes out clean, 35 to 45 minutes.

7. Let the cake cool in the pan on a rack, then use the parchment paper to lift the cake out and onto the rack to cool completely. Store loosely covered at room temperature for up to 2 days or a few days longer in the fridge.

(recipe continues)

Flavor Variations

PISTACHIO CARDAMOM CREAM CHEESE COFFEE CAKE: In the crumble, substitute an equal amount of pistachios for the walnuts and add 1 teaspoon cardamom along with the cinnamon.

BERRY CREAM CHEESE COFFEE CAKE: Sprinkle ½ cup (70g) fresh blueberries over the crumble when you add the cream cheese. Top with the remaining batter and sprinkle with another ½ cup (70g) blueberries before you add the final half of the walnut crumble.

WALNUT SPICE COFFEE CAKE: To the cake batter, add 2 teaspoons cinnamon, 1 teaspoon ground cardamom, and ½ teaspoon freshly grated nutmeg when you add the sour cream and melted butter. Omit the cream cheese, but layer the batter and crumble as directed.

Use Another Pan

ROUND: Bake in a 9-inch round pan until puffed and a tester inserted into the center comes out clean, 40 to 50 minutes.

SHEET: Double the ingredients for the crumble, batter, and cream cheese. Layer as directed in a 9 × 13-inch pan and bake until puffed and a tester inserted into the center comes out clean, 35 to 45 minutes.

Berry Bran Cake

I can rarely resist a big cakey grocery store muffin, and when given the opportunity I always go for a controversial choice: raisin bran. Wheat bran and a bit of whole wheat flour add a wonderful nutty flavor and nubbly texture that I find irresistible. Truth be told, I think I might like the apple and raisin version of this cake a little more, but berries probably have more fans so that is what I've used here. Blackberries work just as nicely as the blueberries.

¾ cup (150g) packed
light brown sugar

2 large eggs

¾ cup (165g) buttermilk

½ cup (95g) neutral oil

1 teaspoon vanilla extract

½ teaspoon fine sea salt

1 teaspoon baking powder

½ teaspoon baking soda

1 cup (128g) all-purpose flour

½ cup (65g) whole wheat flour

½ cup (35g) wheat bran

1½ cups (210g) fresh blueberries

1. Position a rack in the center of the oven and preheat to 350°F. Coat an 8 × 8-inch baking pan with cooking spray or brush with oil. Line the pan with a strip of parchment paper that hangs over two of the edges.

2. In a large bowl, whisk the brown sugar and eggs until pale and foamy, about 1 minute. Add the buttermilk, oil, vanilla, and salt and whisk until smooth and emulsified.

3. Whisk in the baking powder and baking soda. Fold in the all-purpose flour, whole wheat flour, and wheat bran with a spatula and mix until a few streaks of flour remain. Fold in 1 cup (140g) of the blueberries.

4. Pour the batter into the prepared pan and smooth the top. Sprinkle the remaining ½ cup (70g) blueberries over the top.

5. Bake the cake until puffed and golden and a tester inserted into the center comes out clean or with a bit of berry juice, 40 to 45 minutes.

6. Let the cake cool in the pan on a rack for about 15 minutes, then use the parchment paper to lift the cake out and onto the rack to cool completely. Store loosely covered at room temperature for up to 3 days.

Flavor Variations

APPLE AND RAISIN BRAN CAKE: Substitute 1 chopped peeled apple and ½ cup (70g) raisins for the berries and add 1½ teaspoons cinnamon when you add the buttermilk.

BERRY OATMEAL CAKE: Substitute an equal amount of quick-cooking oats for the wheat bran.

CHOCOLATE CHIP BRAN CAKE: Substitute 1 cup (170g) chocolate chips, any type you like, for the blueberries, reserving ⅓ cup (55g) to sprinkle over the top before baking.

Use Another Pan

MUFFINS/CUPCAKES: Line a muffin tin with paper liners and fill the cups two-thirds full. Bake until puffed and a tester inserted into the center comes out clean, about 20 minutes. Makes 12 to 18 muffins/cupcakes.

LOAF: Bake in a 9 × 5 × 3-inch loaf pan until puffed and golden brown and a tester inserted into the center comes out clean, 40 to 50 minutes.

Mocha Banana Cake

Chocolate, coffee, and banana are a harmonious trio in this gorgeously moist cake. It stands up just fine on its own, but the mocha glaze is a beautiful and delicious addition.

Chocolate Banana Cake

1 cup (250g) mashed very ripe banana (about 2 medium bananas)

¾ cup (150g) organic cane sugar

½ cup (110g) unsweetened nondairy milk, any kind

½ cup (95g) neutral oil

2 teaspoons apple cider vinegar

½ teaspoon fine sea salt

½ cup (45g) Dutch process cocoa powder, sifted if lumpy

1 teaspoon baking powder

½ teaspoon baking soda

1½ cups (190g) all-purpose flour

Mocha Glaze

1 cup (100g) organic powdered sugar

1 tablespoon Dutch process cocoa powder

1 tablespoon (14g) nondairy butter, melted

1 teaspoon instant espresso powder

1 to 2 tablespoons unsweetened nondairy milk, any kind

Pinch of salt

1. Position a rack in the center of the oven and preheat to 350°F. Coat an 8 × 8-inch baking pan with cooking spray or brush with oil. Line the pan with a strip of parchment paper that hangs over two of the edges.

2. **MAKE THE CAKE:** In a large bowl, whisk the banana, cane sugar, milk, oil, vinegar, and salt until well combined. Whisk in the cocoa powder until smooth.

3. Whisk in the baking powder and baking soda. Add the flour and whisk until well combined. The batter will be thick.

4. Spoon the batter into the prepared pan and spread in an even layer. Tap the pan on the counter a few times to settle the batter in the pan.

5. Bake the cake until puffed and golden and a tester inserted into the center comes out clean, 35 to 45 minutes.

6. Let the cake cool in the pan on a rack for about 15 minutes, then use the parchment paper to lift the cake out and onto the rack to cool completely.

7. **MAKE THE GLAZE:** When the cake is cool, in a large bowl, combine the powdered sugar, cocoa powder, melted butter, espresso powder, 1 tablespoon milk, and salt and whisk until smooth. Add more milk if necessary to make a thick but pourable glaze.

8. Pour the glaze over the cake and let it set for about 15 minutes before slicing. Store loosely covered at room temperature for up to 3 days. The glaze will soften as it sits.

(recipe continues)

Flavor Variation

CHOCOLATE BANANA CAKE: Fold 1 cup (170g) chopped chocolate into the batter and sprinkle an additional ¼ cup (35g) over the top before baking. Omit the glaze.

Use Another Pan

MUFFINS/CUPCAKES: Line a muffin tin with paper liners and fill the cups two-thirds full. Bake until puffed and a tester inserted into the center comes out clean, about 20 minutes. Makes 12 to 18 muffins/cupcakes.

LOAF: Bake in a 9 × 5 × 3-inch loaf pan until puffed and golden brown and a tester inserted into the center comes out clean, 40 to 50 minutes

Apricot Coconut Cake

Apricots are the unsung heroes of the summer stone fruit crop. They are tart, sweet, a little bit floral, and they slump so beautifully but hold their shape when baked. Just about any stone fruit or berry would make a great substitute for the apricots, and you can add a bit of citrus zest here to brighten the flavors even more.

¾ cup (150g) plus 1 tablespoon granulated sugar

2 large eggs

1 cup (230g) whole-milk ricotta

½ cup (95g) neutral oil

1 teaspoon vanilla extract

½ teaspoon fine sea salt

1½ teaspoons baking powder

½ teaspoon baking soda

1¼ cups (160g) all-purpose flour

¾ cup (68g) unsweetened finely shredded coconut

2½ cups quartered (or halved if small) fresh apricots (4 to 6 apricots)

1. Position a rack in the center of the oven and preheat to 350°F. Coat an 8 × 8-inch baking pan with cooking spray or brush with oil. Line the pan with a strip of parchment paper that hangs over two of the edges.

2. In a large bowl, whisk ¾ cup (150g) of the sugar and the eggs until pale and foamy, about 1 minute. Add the ricotta, oil, vanilla, and salt and whisk until smooth and emulsified.

3. Whisk in the baking powder and baking soda. Fold in the all-purpose flour and ½ cup (50g) of the coconut with a spatula until well mixed.

4. Spoon the batter into the prepared pan and smooth the top. Arrange the apricots evenly over the top; they should almost cover the surface of the cake, with a little bit of batter in between the pieces. Sprinkle the remaining ¼ cup (25g) coconut over the top, then sprinkle with the remaining 1 tablespoon sugar.

5. Bake the cake until puffed and golden and a tester inserted into the center comes out clean or with a few moist crumbs, 50 to 60 minutes.

6. Let the cake cool in the pan on a rack for about 15 minutes, then use the parchment paper to lift the cake out and onto the rack to cool completely. Store loosely covered at room temperature for up to 3 days.

Flavor Variations

BERRY COCONUT CAKE: Substitute 1 cup (140g) blueberries or blackberries for the apricots.

PLUM COCONUT CAKE: Substitute an equal quantity of fresh plums for the apricots.

Use Another Pan

ROUND: Bake in a 9-inch round pan until puffed and a tester inserted into the center comes out clean, 50 to 60 minutes.

Not Quite Texas Sheet Cake

Texas sheet cake is its own category: usually a light, thin chocolate cake topped with a cooked gooey chocolate icing and chopped pecans. It is certainly a party cake and most often baked in a large sheet pan. This cake celebrates all of those same flavors in a smaller and pudgier format.

Chocolate Buttermilk Cake

1 cup (200g) granulated sugar

2 large eggs

¾ cup (165g) buttermilk

½ cup (95g) neutral oil

1 teaspoon vanilla extract

½ teaspoon fine sea salt

½ cup (45g) Dutch process cocoa powder, sifted if lumpy

1 teaspoon baking powder

½ teaspoon baking soda

1¼ cups (160g) all-purpose flour

Chocolate Pecan Topping

6 tablespoons (85g) unsalted butter

¼ cup (23g) Dutch process cocoa powder, sifted if lumpy

2 tablespoons milk

1¼ cups (125g) powdered sugar

Pinch of salt

½ cup (55g) chopped toasted pecans

1. Position a rack in the center of the oven and preheat to 350°F. Coat an 8 × 8-inch baking pan with cooking spray or brush with oil. Line the pan with a strip of parchment paper that hangs over two of the edges.

2. MAKE THE CAKE: In a large bowl, whisk the granulated sugar and eggs until pale and foamy, about 1 minute. Add the buttermilk, oil, vanilla, and salt and whisk until smooth and emulsified.

3. Whisk in the cocoa powder until smooth. Whisk in the baking powder and baking soda. Fold in the flour with a spatula and mix until combined.

4. Pour the batter into the prepared pan and smooth the top.

5. Bake the cake until puffed and a tester inserted into the center comes out clean, 30 to 35 minutes.

6. Let the cake cool in the pan on a rack for about 15 minutes, then use the parchment paper to lift the cake out and onto the rack to cool slightly.

7. MEANWHILE, MAKE THE TOPPING: While the cake is cooling, in a small saucepan, melt the butter. Add the cocoa and whisk until smooth. Remove from the heat and whisk in the milk, powdered sugar, and salt until smooth.

8. Pour the topping over the cake in the pan—it's okay if it is slightly warm—and sprinkle the pecans over the top. Enjoy it right away for maximum gooeyness or let cool until the topping is set, about 20 more minutes, before serving. Store loosely covered at room temperature or in the fridge for about 3 days.

Use Another Pan

ROUND: Bake in a 9-inch round pan until puffed and a tester inserted into the center comes out clean, 30 to 35 minutes.

Lemon Almond Poppy Seed Cake

I love a poppy seed baked good—give me all of your crunchy poppy seed cookies, lemon muffins, cakes, and crackers. This sweet little cake combines two of poppy seeds' best friends: lemon and almond. It has a bit of almond flour for a gorgeous nubbly texture and a layer of crackly lemon glaze for a little pucker. This is also wonderful for dessert with some fresh fruit and cream.

Poppy Seed Cake

2 lemons

¾ cup (150g) granulated sugar

2 large eggs

½ cup (115g) sour cream

½ cup (95g) neutral oil

2 tablespoons lemon juice

2 tablespoons poppy seeds

1 teaspoon almond extract

½ teaspoon fine sea salt

1 teaspoon baking powder

¼ teaspoon baking soda

1½ cups (190g) all-purpose flour

½ cup (50g) almond flour

Lemon Almond Glaze

1 cup (100g) powdered sugar

4 to 6 teaspoons lemon juice

A few drops of almond extract

Pinch of salt

1. Position a rack in the center of the oven and preheat to 350°F. Coat an 8 × 8-inch baking pan with cooking spray or brush with oil. Line the pan with a strip of parchment paper that hangs over two of the edges.

2. **MAKE THE CAKE:** Zest the lemons into a large bowl and add the sugar and eggs and whisk until pale and foamy, about 1 minute. Add the sour cream, oil, lemon juice, poppy seeds, almond extract, and salt and whisk until smooth and emulsified.

3. Whisk in the baking powder and baking soda. Fold in the all-purpose flour and almond flour with a spatula and mix to combine.

4. Pour the batter into the prepared pan and smooth the top.

5. Bake the cake until puffed and golden and a tester inserted into the center comes out clean, 30 to 35 minutes.

6. Let the cake cool in the pan on a rack for about 15 minutes, then use the parchment paper to lift the cake out and onto the rack to cool completely.

7. **MAKE THE GLAZE:** When the cake is cool, in a large bowl, combine the powdered sugar, 4 teaspoons lemon juice, the almond extract, and salt and whisk until smooth. Add more lemon juice as necessary to make a thick but pourable glaze.

8. Pour the glaze over the cake and let it set for about 20 minutes before slicing. Store loosely covered at room temperature for up to 3 days. The glaze will soften as it sits.

(recipe continues)

Flavor Variations

CITRUS ALMOND POPPY SEED CAKE: Substitute an equal amount of orange, lime, grapefruit, or a combination of a few types of citrus for the lemon.

BLACKBERRY ALMOND POPPY SEED CAKE: Sprinkle ¾ cup (105g) fresh blackberries over the batter just before you bake it.

Use Another Pan

MUFFINS/CUPCAKES: Line a muffin tin with paper liners and fill the cups two-thirds full. Bake until puffed and a tester inserted into the center comes out clean, about 20 minutes. Makes 12 to 18 muffins/cupcakes.

LOAF: Bake in a 9 × 5 × 3-inch loaf pan until puffed and golden brown and a tester inserted into the center comes out clean, 40 to 50 minutes.

Nutty Parsnip Cake

Think of parsnips as a funkier carrot. Their sweet and earthy flavor pairs beautifully with spice and nuts. If you can't find parsnips, grated carrots or grated sweet potato are great substitutes. Here, the grated vegetable is matched with a little bit of apple, which makes a perfectly tasty and moist cake that isn't too sweet. Toast the walnuts while the oven is heating to save yourself a little prep time. Add a handful of golden raisins, too, if you like.

½ cup (100g) packed light brown sugar

¼ cup (50g) granulated sugar

2 large eggs

½ cup (95g) neutral oil

1 teaspoon ground cinnamon

½ teaspoon freshly grated nutmeg

¼ teaspoon ground allspice

½ teaspoon fine sea salt

1½ teaspoons baking powder

½ teaspoon baking soda

1¼ cups (160g) all-purpose flour

2 cups (150g) coarsely grated peeled parsnips (about 2 large parsnips)

½ cup (75g) coarsely grated peeled apple

¾ cup (83g) finely chopped toasted walnuts

1. Position a rack in the center of the oven and preheat to 350°F. Coat an 8 × 8-inch baking pan with cooking spray or brush with oil. Line the pan with a strip of parchment paper that hangs over two of the edges.

2. In a large bowl, whisk the brown sugar, granulated sugar, and eggs until pale and foamy, about 1 minute. Add the oil, cinnamon, nutmeg, allspice, and salt and whisk until smooth and emulsified.

3. Whisk in the baking powder and baking soda. Fold in the all-purpose flour with a spatula until a few streaks of flour remain. Fold in the parsnips, apple, and ½ cup (55g) of the walnuts.

4. Spoon the batter into the prepared pan and smooth the top. Sprinkle the remaining ¼ cup (28g) walnuts over the top.

5. Bake the cake until puffed and golden and a tester inserted into the center comes out clean, 30 to 40 minutes.

6. Let the cake cool in the pan on a rack for about 15 minutes, then use the parchment paper to lift the cake out and onto the rack to cool completely. Store loosely covered at room temperature for up to 3 days.

Flavor Variations

NUTTY CARROT CAKE: Substitute an equal amount of shredded carrots for the parsnip. If you'd like, also substitute an equal amount of pecans for the walnuts.

NUTTY ZUCCHINI LIME CAKE: Substitute an equal amount of shredded and gently squeezed zucchini for the parsnip. Drizzle with the lime glaze from Strawberry Lime Almond Cake (page 166) or make the glaze with lemon instead.

Use Another Pan

MUFFINS/CUPCAKES: Line a muffin tin with paper liners and fill the cups two-thirds full. Bake until puffed and a tester inserted into the center comes out clean, about 20 minutes. Makes 12 to 18 muffins/cupcakes.

SHEET: Make a double batch of the batter and bake in a 9 × 13-inch pan until puffed and a tester inserted into the center comes out clean, 40 to 50 minutes.

Use Another Pan

MUFFINS/CUPCAKES: Line a muffin tin with paper liners and fill the cups two-thirds full. Bake until puffed and a tester inserted into the center comes out clean, about 20 minutes. Makes 12 to 18 muffins/cupcakes.

SHEET: Make a double batch of the batter and bake in a 9 × 13-inch pan until puffed and a tester inserted into the center comes out clean, 45 to 55 minutes.

Chocolate Prune Cake

MAKES ONE 8 × 8-INCH CAKE

Prunes have a bad rep, but they are one of my very favorite dried fruits. They are juicy, soft, and molasses-y sweet, and they add a wonderful layer of flavor and moisture to this chocolate cake. If you keep orange liqueur in the house, a couple of tablespoons of it adds additional depth, but you can skip it if you don't have it around.

1 cup (200g) granulated sugar

2 large eggs

1 cup (230g) plain Greek yogurt

½ cup (95g) neutral oil

2 tablespoons Grand Marnier or other orange liqueur (optional)

½ teaspoon fine sea salt

¾ cup (67g) Dutch process cocoa powder, sifted if lumpy

1 teaspoon baking powder

½ teaspoon baking soda

1 cup (128g) all-purpose flour

½ cup (85g) chopped pitted prunes

½ cup (85g) semisweet chocolate chips or chopped chocolate

Powdered sugar (optional), for dusting

1. Position a rack in the center of the oven and preheat to 350°F. Coat an 8 × 8-inch baking pan with cooking spray or brush with oil. Line the pan with a strip of parchment paper that hangs over two of the edges.

2. In a large bowl, whisk the granulated sugar and eggs until pale and foamy, about 1 minute. Add the yogurt, oil, orange liqueur (if using), and salt and whisk until smooth and emulsified.

3. Whisk in the cocoa powder until smooth. Whisk in the baking powder and baking soda. Fold in the flour with a spatula and mix until a few streaks of flour remain. Fold in the prunes and chocolate until well combined.

4. Pour the batter into the prepared pan and smooth the top.

5. Bake the cake until puffed with a few cracks around the edges and a tester inserted into the center comes out clean, 35 to 45 minutes.

6. Let the cake cool in the pan on a rack for about 15 minutes, then use the parchment paper to lift the cake out and onto the rack to cool completely. If desired, dust with powdered sugar before serving. Store loosely covered at room temperature for up to 3 days.

Flavor Variations

BUTTER RUM PRUNE CAKE: Substitute rum for the orange liqueur in the batter. Top the cooled cake with a double batch of the butter rum glaze from the Glazed Cookie Butter Bars (page 98).

EXTRA CHOCOLATEY PRUNE CAKE: Omit the powdered sugar and top the cooled cake with a cocoa glaze. To make the cocoa glaze: In a large bowl, whisk together 1 cup (100g) powdered sugar, 3 tablespoons Dutch process cocoa powder, and a pinch of salt. Add 1 tablespoon soft unsalted butter and whisk in 2 tablespoons boiling water. Add more water if necessary until you have a thick, but pourable glaze.

Strawberry Lime Almond Cake

Thinly sliced strawberries adorn this lime-scented almond cake—which is the perfect base for just about any berry or stone fruit if the strawberries at the market aren't looking so hot. The glaze is (always) optional, but I love that extra sweet-tart hit of flavor. Feel free to sub in lemon or Meyer lemon for the lime.

Strawberry Lime Almond Cake

2 limes

¾ cup (150g) plus 2 teaspoons granulated sugar

2 large eggs

8 tablespoons (113g) unsalted butter, melted

½ teaspoon fine sea salt

1½ teaspoons baking powder

½ teaspoon baking soda

1½ cups (190g) all-purpose flour

½ cup (50g) almond flour

1¼ cups (170g) sliced fresh strawberries

Lime Glaze

¾ cup (75g) powdered sugar

3 to 6 teaspoons lime juice

Pinch of salt

1. Position a rack in the center of the oven and preheat to 350°F. Coat an 8 × 8-inch baking pan with cooking spray or brush with butter. Line the pan with a strip of parchment paper that hangs over two of the edges.

2. **MAKE THE CAKE:** In a large bowl, zest the two limes. Separately, juice one lime and reserve the juice for the glaze.

3. Add ¾ cup (150g) of the granulated sugar and the eggs to the bowl with the zest and whisk until pale and foamy, about 1 minute. Add the melted butter and salt and whisk until smooth and emulsified.

4. Whisk in the baking powder and baking soda. Whisk in the all-purpose flour and almond flour.

5. Spoon the batter into the prepared pan and smooth the top. Arrange the strawberries over the top of the batter in a single layer. Sprinkle the remaining 2 teaspoons granulated sugar over the top.

6. Bake the cake until puffed and golden and a tester inserted into the center comes out clean, 40 to 50 minutes.

7. Let the cake cool in the pan on a rack for about 15 minutes, then use the parchment paper to lift the cake out and onto the rack to cool completely.

8. **MEANWHILE, MAKE THE GLAZE:** While the cake is cooling, in a medium bowl, combine the powdered sugar, 3 teaspoons lime juice, and the salt. Whisk until smooth, adding a bit more lime juice to make an opaque but pourable glaze.

9. Drizzle the glaze over the cooled cake and let it set for a few minutes before slicing. Store loosely covered at room temperature for up to 3 days.

(recipe continues)

Flavor Variations

PLUM LEMON ALMOND CAKE: Add an equal amount of lemon zest in place of the lime to the sugar and eggs. Add 1 teaspoon vanilla or almond extract when you add the melted butter. Omit the strawberries and cut 4 to 5 small plums into halves or quarters and place them on the surface of the batter before baking. Use lemon juice instead of lime in the glaze.

BERRY OR CHERRY LIME ALMOND CAKE: Substitute an equal amount of berries or pitted cherries for the strawberries.

MANGO LIME ALMOND CAKE: Substitute 1 large sliced mango for the strawberries.

Use Another Pan

ROUND: Bake in a 9-inch round pan until puffed and a tester inserted into the center comes out clean, 40 to 50 minutes.

Brown Sugar Peach Cake

MAKES ONE 8 × 8-INCH CAKE

Rich from brown butter and crème fraîche, this is a snack that also makes a gorgeous and easy summer dessert. Crème fraîche, which is a cultured cream, is available at many large supermarkets, but if you can't find it, sour cream is a great substitute. This cake is a true summer stunner.

10 tablespoons (142g) cold unsalted butter, cut into tablespoons

¾ cup (150g) packed light brown sugar

2 large eggs

1 teaspoon vanilla extract

½ teaspoon fine sea salt

¾ cup (173g) crème fraîche

1½ teaspoons baking powder

½ teaspoon baking soda

1½ cups (190g) all-purpose flour

2 small peaches, cut into ½-inch wedges

2 teaspoons granulated sugar

1. Position a rack in the center of the oven and preheat to 350°F. Coat an 8 × 8-inch baking pan with cooking spray or brush with butter. Line the pan with a strip of parchment paper that hangs over two of the edges.

2. In a small skillet or saucepan with a light-colored interior, melt 8 tablespoons (113g) of the butter over medium heat. Once melted, cook the butter, stirring constantly until the milk solids are deep golden brown, about 3 minutes.

3. In a large bowl, combine the brown butter, the remaining 2 tablespoons (29g) cold butter, and the brown sugar. Whisk until the butter melts. The mixture will be a bit grainy and separated. Add the eggs, vanilla, and salt and whisk for about 1 minute. Add the crème fraîche and whisk until emulsified.

4. Whisk in the baking powder and baking soda. Fold in the flour with a spatula and mix until smooth.

5. Spoon the batter into the prepared pan and smooth the top. Arrange the peach wedges over the top of the batter in a single layer (you may have a few extra slices). Sprinkle the granulated sugar over the peaches.

6. Bake the cake until puffed and golden and a tester inserted into the center comes out clean or with a bit of moisture from the fruit, 40 to 45 minutes.

7. Let the cake cool in the pan on a rack for about 15 minutes, then use the parchment paper to lift the cake out and onto the rack to cool completely. Store loosely covered in the fridge for up to 3 days.

Flavor Variations

BROWN SUGAR PEACH AND THYME CAKE: Strip the leaves from 3 thyme sprigs into a large bowl. Make the brown butter, pour the hot butter over the thyme, and let the mixture sit for 1 minute. Add the additional 2 tablespoons (29g) cold butter and the brown sugar and whisk to combine. Proceed with the recipe as written.

BROWN SUGAR APPLE CAKE: Substitute 1 thinly sliced peeled apple for the peaches.

BROWN SUGAR BERRY CAKE: Substitute 1 cup (170g) berries for the peaches.

Use Another Pan

ROUND: Bake in a 9-inch round pan until puffed and golden and a tester inserted into the center comes out clean, 40 to 45 minutes.

SHEET: Make a double batch of the batter and double the peaches and granulated sugar. Bake in a 9 × 13-inch pan until puffed and golden and a tester inserted into the center comes out clean, 45 to 50 minutes.

Mixed-Berry Tahini Cake

MAKES ONE 8 × 8-INCH CAKE

A combination of blueberries, blackberries, and raspberries is delicious in this light and fluffy tahini cake, but any of the three solo is great, too. Make sure to use a high-quality tahini for the best flavor—I love the tahini made by Seed + Mill and Soom.

1 cup (200g) packed
light brown sugar

2 large eggs

½ cup (115g) sour cream

½ cup (100g) tahini, well stirred

½ cup (95g) neutral oil

1 teaspoon vanilla extract

½ teaspoon fine sea salt

1½ teaspoons baking powder

¼ teaspoon baking soda

1½ cups (190g) all-purpose flour

1½ cups (210g) mixed fresh berries (blueberries, blackberries, and raspberries)

1 tablespoon granulated sugar

1. Position a rack in the center of the oven and preheat to 350°F. Coat an 8 × 8-inch baking pan with cooking spray or brush with oil. Line the pan with a strip of parchment paper that hangs over two of the edges.

2. In a large bowl, whisk the brown sugar and eggs until pale and foamy, about 1 minute. Add the sour cream, tahini, oil, vanilla, and salt and whisk until smooth and emulsified.

3. Whisk in the baking powder and baking soda. Fold in the flour and 1 cup (140g) of the berries with a spatula and mix until well combined.

4. Spoon the batter into the prepared pan and smooth the top. Sprinkle the remaining ½ cup (70g) berries and the granulated sugar over the top.

5. Bake the cake until puffed and golden and a tester inserted into the center comes out clean, or with a few moist crumbs, 45 to 55 minutes.

6. Let the cake cool in the pan on a rack for about 15 minutes, then use the parchment paper to lift the cake out and onto the rack to cool completely. Store loosely covered at room temperature for up to 3 days.

Flavor Variation

CHOCOLATE CHIP TAHINI CAKE: Substitute 1 cup (170g) chocolate chips for the berries. Add half to the batter and sprinkle half on top before the cake goes into the oven. Omit the additional granulated sugar sprinkled over the top.

Use Another Pan

LOAF: Bake in a 9 × 5 × 3-inch loaf pan until puffed and golden brown and a tester inserted into the center comes out clean, 50 to 60 minutes.

ROUND: Bake in a 9-inch round pan until puffed and a tester inserted into the center comes out clean, 45 to 55 minutes.

Hummingbird Cake

Pineapple, banana, and pecans are the signature trio of this sweet little cake. Hummingbird cake originated in Jamaica, and it became a runaway hit in the United States shortly after the recipe was published in a magazine in the late 1970s. It is often served with cream cheese frosting, but according to the magazine *Southern Living* it originated as a tube cake, without frosting. Don't worry, though, I wouldn't leave you hanging like that—there's a recipe for cream cheese frosting with the Pink Cookie Bars (page 101).

½ cup (100g) granulated sugar

2 large eggs

½ cup (95g) neutral oil

1 (8-ounce/225g) can juice-packed crushed pineapple, drained (about ¾ cup)

½ cup (125g) mashed very ripe banana (about 1 banana)

½ teaspoon fine sea salt

¼ teaspoon ground cinnamon

¼ teaspoon freshly grated nutmeg

1½ teaspoons baking powder

½ teaspoon baking soda

1½ cups (190g) all-purpose flour

½ cup (55g) chopped toasted pecans

1. Position a rack in the center of the oven and preheat to 350°F. Coat an 8 × 8-inch baking pan with cooking spray or brush with oil. Line the pan with a strip of parchment paper that hangs over two of the edges.

2. In a large bowl, whisk the sugar and eggs until pale and foamy, about 1 minute. Add the oil, pineapple, banana, salt, cinnamon, and nutmeg and stir until combined.

3. Whisk in the baking powder and baking soda. Fold in the flour and ¼ cup (27g) of the pecans with a spatula and mix until well combined.

4. Spoon the batter into the prepared pan and smooth the top. Sprinkle the remaining ¼ cup (27g) pecans over the top.

5. Bake the cake until puffed and golden and a tester inserted into the center comes out clean or with a few moist crumbs, 35 to 40 minutes.

6. Let the cake cool in the pan on a rack for about 15 minutes, then use the parchment paper to lift the cake out and onto the rack to cool completely. Store loosely covered in the fridge for 4 days.

Flavor Variations

HUMMINGBIRD CAKE WITH CREAM CHEESE FROSTING: Omit the ¼ cup (27g) pecans that are sprinkled over the batter before baking (or keep the pecans for garnishing the frosted cake). Make the cream cheese frosting from the Pink Cookie Bars (page 101) but omit the almond extract and add 2 teaspoons lemon juice. A single batch of frosting will be a nice thin layer; a double batch will be more generous. Top the cooled cake with the frosting. Sprinkle the remaining ¼ cup pecans over the frosting.

AUTUMN HUMMINGBIRD CAKE: Substitute an equal amount of unsweetened applesauce for the mashed banana.

Use Another Pan

ROUND: Bake in a 9-inch round pan until puffed and a tester inserted into the center comes out clean, 35 to 40 minutes.

SHEET: Double the ingredients for the batter and the pecan topping and bake in a 9 × 13-inch pan until puffed and a tester inserted into the center comes out clean, 40 to 50 minutes.

Cheesy Jalapeño Corn Bread

This barely honey-sweetened corn bread is packed with lots of pickled jalapeños and cheddar cheese. It's as good on its own as it is next to a bowl of chili, and it's just the thing when you want a treat that hits more cheesy-savory than sweet.

½ cup (70g) pickled jalapeño pepper slices

2 large eggs

¾ cup (165g) buttermilk

8 tablespoons (113g) unsalted butter, melted

¼ cup (75g) mild honey

½ teaspoon fine sea salt

1½ teaspoons baking powder

½ teaspoon baking soda

1 cup (128g) all-purpose flour

½ cup (70g) fine cornmeal

1 cup (100g) shredded sharp cheddar cheese

1. Position a rack in the center of the oven and preheat to 350°F. Coat an 8 × 8-inch baking pan with cooking spray or brush with butter. Line the pan with a strip of parchment paper that hangs over two of the edges.

2. Roughly chop ¼ cup (35g) of the jalapeños.

3. In a large bowl, whisk the eggs, buttermilk, melted butter, honey, and salt until well combined.

4. Whisk in the baking powder and baking soda. Fold in the flour, cornmeal, ½ cup (50g) of the cheddar, and the chopped jalapeños with a spatula and mix until well combined.

5. Spoon the batter into the prepared pan and spread in an even layer. Tap the pan on the counter a few times to settle the batter in the pan. Top with the remaining ¼ cup (35g) jalapeño slices and remaining ½ cup (50g) cheddar.

6. Bake the corn bread until puffed and golden and a tester inserted into the center comes out clean, 25 to 30 minutes.

7. Let the corn bread cool in the pan on a rack for about 15 minutes, then use the parchment paper to lift the cake out and onto the rack to cool completely. Enjoy warm or at room temperature. Store loosely covered at room temperature for up to 3 days.

Flavor Variations

BACON CHEDDAR JALAPEÑO CORN BREAD: Add ¼ cup (20g) crumbled cooked bacon to the batter when you add the cheddar. Sprinkle an additional ¼ cup (20g) bacon over the top before baking.

BLUEBERRY CORN BREAD: Omit the cheese and jalapeños. Fold ½ cup (70g) fresh blueberries into the batter. Sprinkle an additional ½ cup (70g) blueberries over the top before baking.

Use Another Pan

ROUND: Bake in a 9-inch round pan until puffed and a tester inserted into the center comes out clean, 25 to 30 minutes.

Everything Bagel Bread with Scallions

MAKES ONE 8 × 8-INCH PAN

Bagel bread might sound a little confusing but trust me on this one. It is a super-simple buttermilk bread that is endlessly adaptable and perfect for when you need a little savory treat. (Be warned: It's extremely tempting warm from the oven.) You can switch up the mix-ins to your heart's delight and there are a few savory and sweet suggestions that follow (see Flavor Variations, opposite) to get you started. If your everything bagel seasoning blend doesn't contain salt, add a pinch of flaky sea salt to the mix. This also makes an excellent loaf (see Use Another Pan, opposite).

2½ cups (320g) all-purpose flour

2 tablespoons granulated sugar

2 tablespoons everything bagel seasoning

1 tablespoon baking powder

¼ teaspoon fine sea salt

½ cup (40g) thinly sliced scallions or chives

2 ounces (57g) cold cream cheese

1¼ cups (275g) buttermilk, well shaken

9 tablespoons (127g) unsalted butter, melted

1. Position a rack in the center of the oven and preheat to 350°F. Coat an 8 × 8-inch baking pan with cooking spray or brush with butter. Line the pan with a strip of parchment paper that hangs over two of the edges.

2. In a large bowl, stir together the flour, sugar, 1 tablespoon of the everything bagel seasoning, the baking powder, and salt. Add the scallions and stir to coat in the flour. Use your fingers to break up the cream cheese into teaspoon-size pieces and scatter it over the top. Toss to coat in the flour. At this point you can break up the cream cheese pieces a bit more if necessary; it's a little easier when they are coated in flour.

3. Make a well in the center and add the buttermilk and 8 tablespoons (113g) of the melted butter. Gently fold the mixture together until no pockets of flour remain (the dough will be craggy and thick).

4. Spoon the dough into an even layer in the prepared pan and tap the pan on the counter a few times to settle the dough in the pan. It will be lumpy and bumpy. Drizzle the remaining 1 tablespoon melted butter over the top and sprinkle with the remaining 1 tablespoon everything bagel seasoning.

5. Bake the bread until puffed and golden brown and a tester inserted into the center comes out clean, 45 to 55 minutes. The center may be cooked through before the bread is browned; if so, put it back in the oven until it is browned and crusty.

6. Let the bread cool in the pan on a rack for about 15 minutes, then use the parchment paper to lift the bread out and onto the rack to cool slightly. Store loosely covered at room temperature for up to 2 days.

Flavor Variations

SUN-DRIED TOMATO, FETA, AND OLIVE BREAD: Omit the everything bagel seasoning and scallions. Add ¼ cup (40g) chopped sun-dried tomatoes, ¼ cup (40g) chopped pitted kalamata olives, and ¼ cup (40g) crumbled feta cheese.

BERRY BISCUIT BREAD: Omit the everything bagel seasoning and scallions. Add 1 cup (140g) fresh blueberries, blackberries, or a mix of both to the flour mixture before you add the buttermilk and melted butter. Sprinkle 1 tablespoon sugar over the top of the batter before you bake it. A bit of citrus zest or spice would be nice in the batter, too.

Use Another Pan

LOAF: Bake in a 9 × 5 × 3-inch loaf pan until puffed and golden brown and a tester inserted into the center comes out clean, 45 to 55 minutes. The center may be cooked through before the bread is browned; if so, put it back in the oven until it is browned and crusty.

ROUND: Bake in a 9-inch round pan until puffed and a tester inserted into the center comes out clean, 40 to 50 minutes. The center may be cooked through before the bread is browned; if so, put it back in the oven until it is browned and crusty.

make it a sundae!

Turn any snacking bake into a big, bold dessert by adding a scoop of ice cream and a little bit of fancy sauce. These quick sauces come together with just a few ingredients and will last for a while in the fridge. Add some fresh fruit, whipped cream, toasted nuts, or some sprinkles and you have a party on your hands. If sauce is a step too far, just add some ice cream or a bit of whipped cream to your cookie and call it a day.

Salty Caramel Sauce

MAKES ABOUT 2 CUPS

1 cup (200g) granulated sugar

¼ cup (60g) water

¾ teaspoon fine sea salt

8 tablespoons (113g) unsalted butter, cut into tablespoons

½ cup (115g) heavy cream

2 teaspoons vanilla extract or paste

1. In a medium saucepan, combine the sugar, water, and salt. Cook the mixture over medium-high heat, swirling the pan occasionally until the sugar dissolves. Add the butter and cook the mixture, stirring occasionally, until it is deep amber in color, 7 to 10 minutes. The color is more important than the timing here. You want that deep, dark color for the best flavor. Watch the mixture carefully; it will go from perfectly brown to burnt in a flash!

2. Remove from the heat and carefully whisk in the heavy cream. The mixture will foam and bubble, so watch for splatters. Whisk in the vanilla and let the mixture cool slightly before using or storing.

3. When you pour the mixture into a storage container, avoid scraping the sides and bottom of the pan. Sugar crystals may have formed and you don't want them in your caramel. Store in an airtight container in the refrigerator for up to 1 week. Reheat gently in the microwave or in a saucepan over low heat.

Hot Fudge

MAKES ABOUT 2 CUPS

¾ cup (150g) granulated sugar

⅓ cup (30g) Dutch process cocoa powder, sifted if lumpy

¼ teaspoon fine sea salt

1 cup (230g) heavy cream

¼ cup (43g) finely chopped bittersweet chocolate

2 teaspoons vanilla extract or paste

2 tablespoons unsalted butter

1. In a medium saucepan off of the heat, combine the sugar, cocoa, and salt. Whisk until well combined. Slowly stream in the cream while whisking constantly.

2. Bring to a simmer over medium heat, whisking occasionally, and cook until the sugar is melted, about 1 minute. Remove from the heat, then whisk in the chopped chocolate and vanilla until smooth. Whisk in the butter. Put the pan back over low heat and whisk until smooth, about 30 seconds.

3. Let cool to lukewarm before using. Store in an airtight container in the fridge for up to 1 week. Reheat gently in the microwave or in a saucepan over low heat.

Saucy Strawberries

MAKES ABOUT 2 CUPS

I use strawberries here, but you can make saucy blackberries, raspberries, or chopped stone fruit. You can use blueberries, too, but you'll have to mash them with a fork a bit to help them release their juices.

2 cups (320g) sliced strawberries

1 tablespoon sugar, plus more to taste

1 teaspoon vanilla extract or paste

1 teaspoon lemon juice, plus more to taste

In a large bowl, combine the strawberries, sugar, vanilla, and lemon juice. Let sit until the strawberries have released some of their juices and are nice and saucy, about 10 minutes. Taste and adjust the seasoning if necessary, adding a bit more sugar to make it sweeter or lemon juice to cut the sweetness. These are best the day they are made. Store any leftovers in an airtight container in the fridge and use the next day.

(recipe continues)

Some Combinations to Try

- New Favorite Chocolate Chip Cookies (page 61) + vanilla ice cream + Hot Fudge (page 183)

- Brown Butter Marble Cake (page 136) + chocolate ice cream + Hot Fudge (page 183)

- Brown Sugar Peach Cake (page 170) + cinnamon ice cream + Salty Caramel Sauce (page 182)

- Chewy Cocoa Brownies (page 86) + coffee ice cream + Salty Caramel Sauce (page 182)

- Chocolate Ricotta Cake (page 143) + vanilla ice cream + Saucy Strawberries (page 183)

- Coconut Cookie Bark (page 120) + pistachio ice cream + Saucy Strawberries (page 183)

- Glazed Cookie Butter Bars (page 98) + dulce de leche ice cream + Hot Fudge (page 183)

- Do-It-All Salted Butter Shortbread (page 46) + chocolate ice cream + Salty Caramel Sauce (page 182)

- White Chocolate Macadamia Nut Cookies (page 74) + strawberry ice cream + Saucy Strawberries (page 183)

Metric Conversion Chart

1 cup all-purpose flour—128g

1 cup cocoa powder—90g

1 cup granulated sugar—200g

1 cup packed brown sugar—200g

1 cup powdered sugar—100g

1 cup ricotta, sour cream, or yogurt—230g

1 cup chopped nuts—110g

1 cup chopped chocolate or chocolate chips—170g

8 tablespoons (1 stick) butter—113g

acknowledgments

To Pete, my biggest and most enthusiastic supporter, I can't imagine doing any of this without you.

Big, big thanks also goes out to:

My family, who are always available for recipe testing, feedback, cheerleading, and expert advice.

The team at Clarkson Potter: Jenn Sit, Jen Wang, Bianca Cruz, Jessica Heim, Patricia Shaw, Stephanie Huntwork, the marketing and publicity teams, and everyone else who worked on this book behind the scenes for having me back to make *Snacking Cakes* the perfect sibling.

My agent, Kari Stuart, for all of your hard work, counsel, and encouragement.

My photo shoot team, who sweat it out with me on those hot July days: Joy Cho, Nikki Jessop, and Brooke Deonarine. You all baked so many beautiful cookies, bars, and cakes, found beautiful props, and provided excellent tasting notes along the way.

My incredible team of recipe testers: Janet, Mom, Julie, Ali, Kelly, Keira, Liv, Sophy, Yousef, Amy, Jumee, Janie, Saunders, Danielle, Olaiya, MariPat, Andrea, Cathie, Fahren, Molly L., Molly D., Peggy, and Rosie. Your hard work is so crucial, and I appreciate the time and resources you put into helping me make this book so special.

To the generous artists and brands who donated their wares and products for this shoot: Beau Rush, Meilen Ceramics, Opinel, Crow Canyon, Material Kitchen, and Valrhona Chocolate. You made these photos beautiful and delicious!

My emotional support furry friends, Arlo and Abigail. Endless love and scratches for you both.

To the readers and lovers of *Snacking Cakes*, *Sweeter off the Vine*, and *Apt. 2B Baking Co.*, thank you so much for your support over these many years.

index

CLARKSON POTTER is a trademark and POTTER with colophon
is a registered trademark of Penguin Random House LLC.

Photograph on page 187 is courtesy of Zachary Gray

Library of Congress Cataloging-in-Publication Data
is available upon request.

ISBN 978-0-593-57917-6
eBook ISBN 978-0-593-57918-3

Printed in China

Photographer and Food Stylist: Yossy Arefi
Food Stylist Assistants: Joy Cho
and Nikki Jessop
Prop Sourcing: Brooke Deonarine
Editor: Jennifer Sit
Editorial Assistant: Bianca Cruz
Designer: Jen Wang
Production Editor: Patricia Shaw
Production Manager: Jessica Heim
Compositors: Merri Ann Morrell
and Hannah Hunt
Copy Editor: Kate Slate
Indexer: Elizabeth T. Parson
Marketer: Andrea Portanova
Publicist: Erica Gelbard

10 9 8 7 6 5 4 3 2

First Edition